The Essence of Place

Concept and Project Management John Duren

Writing Douglas Wood

Design Martin Skoro and Ross Rezac, MartinRoss Design

Photography, unless stated otherwise, John Duren

Copy Editing Jane St. Anthony

ISBN 978-0-692-59136-9
Library of Congress Catalog Number 2015921088

Printed in Canada

©2016 Jay C. Hormel Nature Center
1304 21st St. NE, Austin, MN 55912
507.437.7519
www.hormelnaturecenter.org
All rights reserved. Published in 2016

The West Prairie awaits a midsummer rainstorm.
Photograph ghosted to 30%

Cover: A blackburnian warbler rests in the treetops during its spring migration.
End sheets: Red pines stretch toward the sky.
Previous Page: Canada geese fly over the Lone Oak Loop at dawn.
Photograph ghosted to 30%

The Essence of Place

THE STORY OF THE JAY C. HORMEL NATURE CENTER

John Duren

Douglas Wood

CONTENTS

Acknowledgements	6
Foreword	7
Preface	8
Chapter 1 From Roots to Fruition: The Origins of a Nature Center	13
Chapter 2 Whose Woods These Are . . .	29
Chapter 3 A Patch Of Prairie— A Poem From the Past	67
Chapter 4 A Pond on the Prairie	111
Chapter 5 Connecting People With the Land: Education, Conservation, Magic	147
Photographer's Notes	193

A bridge spans the south branch of Dobbins Creek.

ACKNOWLEDGEMENTS

First, I would like to thank The Hormel Foundation. The Hormel Foundation contributes annually to a number of different projects in the Austin area and is devoted to the betterment of the community. It was the first organization to get involved in the creation of this book, and that leap of faith got this project moving.

I would also like to thank the Friends of the Jay C. Hormel Nature Center. When I proposed the idea of this book to them and said we would need funding to complete it, there was no hesitation at all. We were off and running.

Thank you to the people who worked incredibly hard to create this book: Douglas Wood, for his wonderful ability to make nature come alive through use of the written word; and Martin Skoro and Ross Rezac of MartinRoss Design, for their immense talent in the art of book design. A special thanks goes to the staff at the Jay C. Hormel Nature Center, Hormel Foods Archives Department, Mower County Historical Society, and Gerard Academy. Each of these places allowed me to look through historical photos and gather information in order to tell the complete story of the nature center.

Also, I would like to thank my parents, Tim and Cathy, for encouraging me to pursue photography and helping me chase my dreams. Words cannot thank you enough. Thank you to Gary and Pat Ray, who believed in me as a photographer before almost anyone else did. Their support and encouragement has meant a lot to me.

I would also like to thank Larry Dolphin for helping me get this project underway and believing that I would get the job done.

While working on this project, there have been many amazing people who have helped along the way. Thank you to everyone who played a part in creating this book. It was truly a team effort.

—John Duren

As the writer of this book, I would particularly like to acknowledge John Duren for his inspiration, artistry, and gumption in making it happen; for countless hours spent stalking "just the right shot." You got them, John. And as this publication roughly marks the conclusion of Director Larry Dolphin's tenure, I'd like to congratulate him for his lasting and profound impact upon the center, upon a particular portion of the earth, and upon the people of Austin, Minnesota.

—Douglas Wood

A palm warbler perches in the marshy vegetation near the pond.
Photograph ghosted to 20%

FOREWORD

Every place of significance is more than just itself. It is more than the rise and fall of the land, more than the way it smells on an August morning or an Indian summer afternoon, more than the way the snow piles up when the January winds howl out of the northwest. It is more than the sunlight glinting off a favorite riffle or the scarlet tones of a cardinal from a tall tree. It is more than all the various species of plants and animals that call it home.

Each of these things helps to define a place, to compose a landscape, to make it what it is. But there is something beyond all of this. A sense of place, to be complete, also has to do with all that has been brought or given to a landscape by those who love and care for it. It has to do with the long gathering of dreams and aspirations, sweat and tears. It involves the bonds of affection and appreciation that a place inspires, and that accumulate through the years and the generations, becoming as much a part of it as spring wildflowers and the leaves that decompose in the fall. These intangible things profoundly affect the meaning of a place, and become themselves a part of the deep and lasting story of any piece of the earth.

Meanwhile, the land itself becomes a part of the people who love it, a part of the very soil and bedrock of their lives. The stories of those people become so interwoven into the story of the land, the tapestry of it, that at some point the two can no longer be separated, one from the other.

A place of significance is a place with a story. The Jay C. Hormel Nature Center is such a place.

—Douglas Wood

PREFACE

I was ready to go home. After spending most of the day hiking at the Jay C. Hormel Nature Center, I was still without a shot. Actually, I hadn't even taken the camera off my shoulder. As the late October sun began its descent, I started walking to my car. A large part of me wanted to be done for the day. After all, wildlife photography was just a hobby for me in 2009. I didn't have to be there. Something inside of me, however, told me to stay. Begrudgingly, I obliged and ten minutes later found myself sitting in the south pines watching the shadows of the trees dance across the forest floor.

Wildlife photography can be a test of the will. People think that you must have patience to get shots of wild animals; I disagree. For me it's about persistence. There are more than a few definitions of the word, and the ones I like the best are "enduring tenaciously" and "persisting in spite of opposition." I like to think both of these adequately describe my work as a wildlife photographer, but there is one definition that does so more: "constantly repeated."

As I sat under the canopy of pines, I leaned back and closed my eyes. It had been a long day and I was tired. I had no intention of sleeping, but I felt myself slowly start to drift off. Not wanting to miss anything, I forced myself to stay awake and keep vigilant. Just a few days ago I had taken a nice shot of a sizable doe in the same spot I was sitting now. Hopefully, a big buck would wander by.

The sun continued to lessen in intensity. As it shown through the trees, there became fewer and fewer spots where it was hitting the ground. If I were to get an image now, the animal would have to be in the right spot at the right time. Still sitting on the ground, leaning against a tree, I knew that the odds were against me for getting any shots that evening.

One of the parts about wildlife photography that I enjoy the most is picking a spot in the middle of a forest, prairie, wetland, or any other type of habitat, and just sitting there, waiting. When sitting in silence in a wild place, you become a part of that environment. When this happens, the true essence of the place can be felt. Long-time nature center director Larry Dolphin once told me a story about sleeping in the woods and waking up to find a ruffed grouse walking across his legs. These stories only happen when we embrace silence.

Facing south and sitting only a hundred yards from Interstate 90, the sounds of freeway traffic had been serenading me for the last hour. As I scanned my immediate surroundings, I saw nothing but a few downed trees. Just before standing up, I peered around the tree that I had been lazily resting on and saw something. Actually, it was two things. Two gray animals were forty yards north of me, sitting in a thicket and much too far away for me to get any type of quality image.

Thinking at best they were woodchucks and at worst they were stray cats, I began to move closer. Leaves crunched beneath my feet: thirty yards. I kept low and as unimposing as possible: twenty yards. When I got closer, I realized what they were: two gray foxes. Upon the realization that the animals

I was looking at were not woodchucks or cats but foxes, I tempered my steps. But it was too late; I had been spotted. One of the animals darted west and was out of sight in an instant. The other, surprisingly, stayed put. Expecting the remaining fox to follow the example of the one that fled, I paused and crouched down toward the earth.

For what seemed liked ages we looked at each other, the fox perhaps more calm than the photographer. Slowly standing up, I continued my approach. Now within fifteen yards, I dropped to a knee and took a shot. The sound of the shutter didn't seem to bother the animal, and I was able to capture several frames. At last, after posing nicely for a portrait and seeming to smile as well, the fox got up and walked east into the shadows.

At the moment I took that picture, this book project began. Officially, it started in December 2014.

Within this book are thousands of hours of photographs. Some took hours, some took days. Some show the beauty of life, some show the harshness of death. All, however, tell a story. My hope is that the images in this book captivate and inspire you, open up your sense of wonder, and incite your imagination. As Albert Einstein said, "He who can no longer pause to wonder . . . is as good as dead; his eyes are closed." Let us walk with eyes open.

—John Duren

A gray fox pauses to rest among the south pines.

A maple leaf clings to a rock in Dobbins Creek.

I only went out for a walk and finally concluded to stay out till sundown, for going out, I found, was really going in.

—John Muir

CHAPTER 1

From Roots to Fruition: The Origins of a Nature Center

In the late 1920s, a young man from Austin, Minnesota, named Jay Hormel decided he wanted to create an arboretum. As a child, he had loved to play in a grove of trees that had since disappeared. The grove lingered fondly in his memory, and it was his heart's desire to recreate such a place of shaded beauty for himself and for others to enjoy.

So it was that a piece of southern Minnesota land began its long transformation from plowed creekside prairie in the great oak savanna to the varied and wooded landscape of the Jay C. Hormel Nature Center that people know today.

Jay Hormel was the only child of George and Lillian Hormel. George was a highly successful and prosperous businessman who had founded the Geo. A. Hormel & Co. meat packing company in 1891. Born in 1892, Jay grew up in the family "mansion" in Austin. The house was originally built in 1871 by John Cook, prominent businessman and former mayor of Austin. The Hormels bought the home in 1901 and began extensive remodeling and renovation, including a cantilevered roof and large white columns, creating a Greek Revival style of architecture. Photos of the time reflect the startling transformation. The Hormel home was a hub of activity in the small town of Austin, hosting countless social and cultural gatherings, business and stockholder meetings. The house can still be seen and enjoyed today. As the Hormel Historic Home, it was restored and reorganized in 1992, to provide guided tours and reservations for special events.

Jay grew up in this house, from the age of nine. He cherished memories of playing among the trees in the yard. His bedroom upstairs included a small sunroom or alcove entered by a low doorway. There his windows looked out over the town of Austin, the community upon which his father and mother had such an impact.

The packing company that his father founded was established at an abandoned creamery. Stories of George A. Hormel, his accomplishments and philosophy of life were legion. He was always "at the plant" by seven o'clock in the morning, usually arriving with "Billy," his strawberry roan carriage horse. Word was that if Lillian Hormel needed the horse while it was at the plant, George would leave a note on its back for anyone to read, saying, "Let him go." When Billy was let loose, he went straight home.

A 1917 article in southern Minnesota's *Fairmont Sentinel* read, "What one man can do for a town is illustrated in Austin where George A. Hormel has built up a packing establishment that has done a business of $14 million during the past year. Mr. Hormel is a public-spirited, enterprising citizen, and a booster for every good cause. Austin and southern Minnesota are beneficiaries of his remarkable talent for organizing and developing a great business."

Top: Jay's childhood home before renovations
Photo courtesy of Hormel Historic Home

Bottom: The Hormel Historic Home as it sits today.

Opposite: An aerial view of the Jay C. Hormel Nature Center

CHAPTER 1

Of his business philosophy, George said, "I kept constantly before me the challenge, 'Originate, don't imitate!' and made it one of the commandments of the organization."

This demanding personal ethic was perhaps inherited from George's father, of whom he said, "I could see in terms of my own experience what Father meant: Men . . . were often less handicapped by circumstances than they were by poverty of thought and their inability to grasp the fact that they were masters of their own destiny."

Yet this unflinching work ethic and personal code were balanced, by all accounts, with a sense of empathy and appreciation for others.

Jay Hormel's childhood bedroom

CHAPTER 1

Regarding business, George Hormel said, "I incessantly preached that we were engaged in one of the most important tasks in the world . . . feeding people. Nothing that contributed to the quality of their food was too much trouble."

There were other examples of human warmth and concern for others in this hard-nosed, turn-of-the-century business tycoon. George had occasion to build a stable during hard economic times. Out of concern for the community, George insisted that all the men building it should be married with children. A slot machine was at one time ensconced within the house, but never paid out a jackpot. Instead, all the money going in went back out to area schools to pay for milk and other necessities.

Of Lillian, his wife, he said, "My wife stood guard on the homefront. She was patient and unruffled at times when there was enough tension in the house to blow off the roof. My nerves were raw from the pressures placed upon me. At times when the strain seemed greater than I could bear, her support and belief were of inestimable value. She never doubted that we would come through."

And years later, regarding a final act of generosity, Lillian Hormel herself wrote, "It became apparent that if (George) was to keep up his health, he must give up the wearing grind of the details of his work at the plant, and to do this he must spend more time away from Austin, so we decided to build in California. Then the question arose as to what to do with our home here, and we decided that we could get no more pleasure out of it than to see it made use of by the girls of this city." Thus the elegant property was donated to the YWCA, with the bedrooms inexpensively rented out to young single women.

This, then, was the Austin childhood of young Jay Hormel—life in a community showplace and center of social and business activity, with parents who valued both the pursuit of success and a community-minded concern for others. They were lessons that Jay took to heart.

Jay showed a head for business early on, when as a young boy he left cans with Austin house-wives in which they could gather cooking grease. Later he collected the cans, paid the housewives a fee, and resold the grease to the packing house. Jay attended Shattuck Academy in nearby Faribault, and later, Princeton University. After moving back home to work at the company, he was the fourth drafted man to report to Camp Dodge, Iowa, for World War I.

As an officer in a meat refrigeration company in France, he recommended that all the beef be "boned out" to save on cargo space. His superiors responded by sending him back to the U.S. to work out a plan for the entire service, which resulted in vast savings of cargo space.

George and Lillian Hormel
Photo provided by
Hormel Foods Corporation.

CHAPTER 1

Returning to France in 1922, Jay married Germaine Dubois, the beautiful daughter of a miller, with whom he had fallen in love as a soldier. Three sons were eventually born to the couple—George, Thomas, and James.

Jay returned to work for his father's business. Under his direction, Geo. A. Hormel & Co. perfected the canning of hams in 1926. (This led to further research and innovation, finally resulting in 1937 in a consumer-sized can of ground and spiced pork called SPAM® luncheon meat, a product that became a part of American history.) In 1927, with his parents' move to California, Jay became head of the company, in many ways carrying on his father's vision of hard work and community involvement. He oversaw further innovations such as canned chili. In addition, he became widely known in business circles for his forward-thinking policies on employment. In an industry and a time of seasonal, boom-and-bust hiring practices, Jay Hormel was one of the first to promote and practice an annual wage plan. This steady, year-round employment had a positive effect on the Austin community. Students and newspaper and magazine reporters from far and wide came to Austin to study the phenomenon of stable employment practices.

Jay Hormel's business philosophy could perhaps be summed up by a statement to his salesmen: "Business does not exist apart from humanity. Business is a vehicle for giving—a vehicle for getting and giving."

It was also in about 1927, the year of his ascension to the presidency of the company, that Jay began to seriously implement his dream of an arboretum, planting trees on his newly acquired property on the east edge of town as an homage to the lost grove of his youth and to the perceived benefit of his community. Some of the first plantings would have been silver poplar, American elm, and Ohio buckeye. As stated by his property manager, Roy Anderson, "Mr. Hormel had a profound love of trees. On several occasions . . . he said that several generations of pioneers and farmers had spent their lives removing the trees and that he expected to spend his getting them back."

The Hormels' new home—on about 250 acres of grain fields and pastures along Dobbins Creek—flowered magnificently, becoming a grand, French-style estate that dwarfed even the stately home of Jay's childhood. Meanwhile, the arboretum, planted on 123 acres, grew as well. Roy Anderson kept a "Tree Book" that documented all plantings, carefully laying out where each species was located. The original goal was to plant every tree native to Minnesota. Eventually that goal was expanded to include trees from all over the country and around the world, species that it was thought could thrive in Minnesota. Anderson estimated that in excess of 200,000 trees were planted over three decades, including 30 different seed sources of jack pine and an experimental shelter belt or windbreak. Said Anderson, "Mr. Hormel felt that too much of southern Minnesota was washing away or blowing away, and that each farm should have the advantage of protection by trees."

Above: Jay and Germaine Hormel
Photo provided by
Hormel Foods Corporation

Opposite top: Dinner menu
Document provided by
Mower County Historical Society

Bottom: Estate of Jay Hormel
Photo provided by Mower County
Historical Society

CHAPTER 1

As the decades passed, Geo. A. Hormel & Co. continued to flourish. The Jay Hormel family grew up and so did many of the trees. Jay Hormel died in 1954, at only 61 years of age. All the stores and offices of Austin were closed for the day of his funeral, and attendees came from as far away as New York and California. The Princeton alumni paper stated, "Princeton has lost an outstanding alumnus, and the nation a leader." His parents, George and Lillian, had preceded him in death in 1946. All three funeral services were held at the old Hormel Historic Home where Jay had grown up.

After Jay's death, George (Geordie) Hormel purchased title to the Jay Hormel estate and transformed the house into a grand restaurant and hotel called the King's Wood Hotel. Billed as "one of the most fabulous hotels and dining places in the country," the King's Wood featured 97 rooms and luxury suites, three dining rooms to accommodate 300 diners, and world-class cuisine. Geordie, a fine musician, often played piano for his guests in the lounge. But in the end, small town Austin could not support such a lavish entertainment center, and the hotel closed in 1962.

CHAPTER 1

CHAPTER 1

In 1963, King's Wood was purchased by a religious order, the Oblate Fathers of St. Paul, as a retreat, again undergoing extensive remodeling for its new role. In 1969, it became the Gerard House, named for St. Gerard, patron saint of children. As a residential treatment center for emotionally disturbed children, it went through various iterations and it remains to this day.

As for the old tree plantings along and north of Dobbins Creek, years without the guiding hand of their benefactor took a toll, and the arboretum fell largely into disuse. There was talk of commercial development on the site. But the story of this piece of land, into which so many hopes and dreams had been sown, was not yet complete.

Along with the trees, seeds had long since been planted for a plot of the earth set aside, a green space that could counterbalance the plowing, paving, and development of 20th-century America. It remained for a new vision and new energy, something beyond the original private arboretum, to help these old seeds grow to fruition.

It was in 1970 that local community leaders, responding to a sense that somehow the land should be preserved, advanced a proposal to purchase a portion of the former Hormel estate. A combination of federal and state funds enabled the purchase of 123 acres. More grant money was found in 1971, including funds from The Hormel Foundation, which allowed the beginnings of limited development, including a parking lot, a pond, bridges, and 2.5 miles of trails. At one point, the Austin City Council proposed the idea of having the state Department of Natural Resources take over the property and operate it as a state park, but this idea was strenuously opposed by much of the community and was rescinded.

Meanwhile, the Austin Parks, Recreation, and Forestry Board created the Jay C. Hormel Nature Center Committee, charged with the responsibility of managing the center, planning development, and finding more funding. The National Audubon Society also aided in some of the preliminary planning.

In 1974, the Ober Charitable Foundation of St. Paul, responding to a grant application, provided funds for construction of an interpretive building and the hiring of a director. This initial construction was done largely by volunteers, under the supervision of Richard Birger, hired as the center's first director. In September of 1975, formal dedication of the center's interpretive building took place, with many dignitaries, including Senator Hubert Humphrey as the main speaker.

As the *Austin Daily Herald* reported on March 30, 1976, "The Jay C. Hormel Nature Center is unique in many respects; one perhaps is the manner in which it came about. The interest of local citizens in preserving a piece of natural land combined with the . . . generosity of two charitable foundations. All of this teamed with the state and federal effort not only to preserve the land but also educate ourselves and our children as to how the natural world functions."

Jay proudly displays his trees.
Photo provided by Hormel Foods Corporation

Opposite: An aerial photo taken in 1952 shows the Hormel estate surrounded by a flourishing forest.
Photo provided by the Jay C. Hormel Nature Center/George Miles Ryan Studios

CHAPTER 1

CHAPTER 1

Vince Shay succeeded Richard Birger as director in 1978. Over the next ten years, the center continued to grow and develop. In 1988, Larry Dolphin began his 27-year tenure as director, a time of tremendous change, community involvement, and advances in preservation and stewardship.

In the decades since the dedication of the center in 1975, much has occurred to add to the meaning and intangible values of this piece of the earth. The generous hearts and hands of many devoted supporters and volunteers have added to its story.

An enormous 3.6 billion-year-old glacial boulder made a belated cross-country journey across an ice road to become a nature center landmark. Hundreds more acres of woods and prairie have been added or restored, and saved from development. A beautiful auditorium was constructed, hosting innumerable concerts and programs. Thousands upon thousands of school children have walked the property's trails and bridges, marveling at its beauties, listening to the sounds of barred owls and jays and cardinals, discovering the mysteries of making maple syrup, and in the process becoming inspired to forge their own connections with the living earth. The photographer of this book, John Duren, fondly credits his own schoolboy visits to the nature center for his inspiration to pursue outdoor photography, leading to the images within these pages. Countless families have joined hands to walk the woods or prairie, or to sit on a footbridge and listen to the music of flowing water. And very soon the erection and dedication of the new visitor center will put the capstone on a long campaign, and provide decades of opportunities for education and enrichment.

One thinks that Jay Hormel would approve these ongoing efforts to manage the land, and at the same time, to impact people in a positive way. In fact, it is not hard to imagine young Jay, an only child and a bit lonely perhaps, gazing out at the world from the high windows of his bedroom alcove, listening to the commotion of the grand social gatherings below, and thinking that someday he, too, would make his mark in the world. It would be a world with plenty of green. A world with a few more trees, perhaps . . .

Opposite: Dobbins Creek flows over the walking path, leaving only the stepping stones visible.
Top: Ruby Rupner Auditorium
Bottom: A digital rendering of the interpretive center gives a preview of the finished building.
Design image provided by I+S Group.

CHAPTER 1

The early morning sun illuminates the lush forest canopy.

CHAPTER 1

1927

Jay C. Hormel Nature Center Timeline

Top: Dining room at King's Wood Hotel
Photographed by Austin Daily Herald, photo provided by Mower County Historical Society

Bottom: This 125-ton gneiss rock was moved one-and-a-half miles to the nature center from nearby Todd Park.

1927 Jay Catherwood Hormel plants the first of more than 200,000 trees that would grow on his property over the next 25 years.

1958 Geordie Hormel purchases title to the Jay C. Hormel estate and opens the King's Wood Hotel.

The Hormel Foundation retains the adjacent arboretum and buildings.

1963 King's Wood Hotel is purchased by the Oblate Fathers of St. Paul as a retreat.

1969 The former Jay C. Hormel estate becomes the Gerard House, a residential treatment center for emotionally disturbed children.

1971 The City of Austin acquires 123 acres of land around the Hormel estate, and the Jay C. Hormel Nature Center is founded.

1973 Wildlife pond is excavated.

1974 Richard Birger is hired as the nature center's first director.

1975 U.S. Senator Hubert Humphrey speaks at the dedication of the nature center's interpretive building.

1976 Dan Clayton becomes the full-time land manager.

1978 Fifty-five acres of land are added to the nature center. Vince Shay replaces Richard Birger as director/naturalist.

1980 "Red," a human-imprinted, male, red-tailed hawk, is acquired for educational purposes.

1984 The nature center expands by 101 acres.

1985 A 125-ton gneiss rock, a glacial erratic, is moved 1.5 miles over snow and ice from Todd Park.

1988 Larry Dolphin replaces Vince Shay as the new director/naturalist.

1989 The Friends of the Jay C. Hormel Nature Center is established.

1992 Margaret Beck makes a sizable donation in memory of her longtime friend Ruby Rupner to establish the Ruby Rupner Auditorium and a series of free environmental programs.

The Jacques Chipault Memorial Handicapped Access Trail is dedicated.

2016

CHAPTER 1

1994 The Ruby Rupner Auditorium is dedicated.

1996 The nature center celebrates its 25th anniversary with guest speaker Nina Leopold Bradley, daughter of Aldo Leopold, author of the *Sand County Almanac* and considered by many to be the father of wildlife management.

1999 Julie Champlin is hired as nature center administrative assistant.

2000 Duane Sucha replaces Dan Clayton as land manager.

2002 The Friends of the Jay C. Hormel Nature Center begins a fundraising campaign to acquire 210 acres, from two property owners, to add land to the north of the tower.

The log cabin is constructed and donated by an anonymous donor.

2003 Sixty-two acres are acquired from Marvin and Lorraine Gaard.

2004 Eight acres are donated to the nature center by David Dickson and James Heimark.

2005 A barred owl is acquired as an educational bird of prey.

2009 Over 350 trees are destroyed and one-third of the visitor center roof is torn off by a tornado.

2010 The nature center takes possession of 148 acres from Wayne Diekrager.

2011 The 40th anniversary is celebrated.

Mike Goetz replaces Duane Sucha as land manager.

2013 Eleven acres are transferred to the City of Austin and the Jay C. Hormel Nature Center from Tom and Susan Hemann.

2014 The Hormel Foundation agrees to give a $5 million grant to help fund the $7 million project to build a new interpretive center.

2015 Eleven acres are acquired from Delmer Ellis.

2016 Construction on the new interpretive center begins.

Top: The nature center's educational bird of prey, "Red," the red-tailed hawk, lived for 35 years.
Middle: The Ruby Rupner Auditorium
Bottom: The log cabin sits just north of the parking lot and was constructed in 2002.

The sun rises over the Jay C. Hormel Nature Center.

The creation of a thousand forests is in one acorn.

—Ralph Waldo Emerson

CHAPTER 2

Whose Woods These Are . . .

*W*hen Jay C. Hormel decided he wanted to plant a woods, an arboretum, he was by all accounts harkening back to the days of his childhood, when a particular woods took hold of his imagination. This is not hard to understand, for forests have captured children's imaginations seemingly forever, from Robert Frost's *A Swinger of Birches* to the Sherwood Forest of Robin Hood; from the American frontier of Davy Crockett and Daniel Boone to the mountain fastness of Kit Carson and Jim Bridger to the African jungles of Burroughs' *Tarzan*; from the dark and scary woods of *Grimm's Fairy Tales* to Maurice Sendak's *Where The Wild Things Are* to the Hundred Acre Wood of *Winnie-the-Pooh*. The imaginations of boys and girls have long thrilled to thoughts and images of the shadowy, mysterious realm of the forest.

Nor is it children alone who harbor such feelings. Americans love deserts and seashores and mountains; still, when they plan or dream of a wilderness outing or a camping trip, it is often to thoughts of "the woods" that they first turn.

Yet our American relationship with the woods is complex. "The groves were God's first temples. . . ," wrote William Cullen Bryant. The historic Hudson Bay School of landscape artists used light and shade and the magic of perspective to portray the Great American Forest in the most romantic of ways. People like Crockett and Boone became legendary folk heroes in their time largely because of their relationship to the woods. Thoreau and Emerson founded a quintessentially American spiritual philosophy based largely on their feelings for the woods.

But there was also a deep strain of fear, of dread and anxiety that saw the woods as a tangled and foreboding place best left alone. Or if not left alone, then subdued and cleared and made suitable for farm and town and civilization. "The plow follows the axe," was the old frontier saying. Thus were great tracts of the American eastern woodlands—an astounding ecosystem where frontiersmen once said a squirrel could run from the Atlantic Ocean to the Mississippi River and never touch the ground—decimated in the name of progress. Thus was the Minnesota white pine forest that loggers said would last forever, gone in about 40 years. Thus we had the Great Hinckley Fire of 1894 and other terrible conflagrations due to poor forestry practices. Thus do we still see tropical rainforests disappearing due to deforestation today. And thus did a small woods near Austin in southern Minnesota vanish from the life of a young boy named Jay Hormel.

So when the adult Jay felt the urge to leave a legacy upon the land, he remembered the lost woods of his youth and determined that he would leave a woods—not just for the child within him, but for the children of future generations who otherwise might never have a woods to walk.

A raccoon peers through the forest foliage.

CHAPTER 2

The Hormel woods that we walk today essentially began in the late 1920s, with plantings for Jay's arboretum. There may have been a few oaks or river bottom trees remaining from earlier days, but surely not many. Under the watchful eye of caretaker Roy Anderson, more than 200,000 trees were planted over a 30-year period. A wonderful, hardbound "Tree Book" compiled by Mr. Anderson survives yet today in the nature center's care, lovingly detailing the history and exact number of plantings, the names of the species, and the layout along Dobbins Creek. On the front-end paper of the book is a fine, hand-drawn map providing an overview.

To hold the old, ten-pound book in your hands, to run your fingers along the frayed corners and study the old diagrams, is to let your imagination return to the days when the forest was only a dream. Now, to walk on a trail under nearly century-old white pines or green ash, is to feel the sense of a dream fulfilled.

According to Mr. Anderson, Jay Hormel said that several generations of farmers had spent their lives removing trees, and he expected to spend his getting them back. And so the plantings proceeded, first on the original 40 acres around his new home, expanding over the years to 123 acres. The first trees planted were silver poplar, Ohio buckeye, and American elm. This modest list eventually expanded to 85 species, including virtually all the Minnesota natives, plus trees from around the country and other parts of the world. Chinese elm, hackberry, Colorado spruce, white spruce, jack pine, wild crab, chokecherry, golden willow, hawthorn, birch, aspen, box elder, black walnut, linden, chestnut, pin oak, and dozens of others are listed in the old book, and many can be seen yet today. Many other species beyond the original 85 were also planted but not documented, as well as ferns, wildflowers, vines, and grasses. It was said to be the finest arboretum in the state, save the University of Minnesota Landscape Arboretum.

But of course, a forest is not diagrams and notes in a book, nor is it even an ambitious series of plantings. A real woods is a feeling, a fragrance, a cool shade on a hot day, shafts of sunlight through a green, arched ceiling, the hoot of a barred owl or the song of a cardinal, the crash of a stag through the shadows. A real woods is what happens over long, slow decades of life and growth and death and decay and rebirth. It is such a complex, interconnected web of life that it cannot be described in words, or even created from a plan. It can be started perhaps, and nurtured and protected, but then it must create itself, must become itself.

That green, arched ceiling is called a canopy, and within it are the high flyers, the creatures that feel at home near the sky. Here are the blue jays and fly-catchers and crows and hawks; here also the gray and red and fox squirrels, leaping from limb to limb. Here the leaves soak up the sunlight and send the accumulated energy far below.

May apples carpet the forest floor in early spring.

Beneath the canopy and its blanket of shade are the understory and the shrub layer. Even more birds and creatures are to be found here, foraging and building nests and homes in a gentler realm,

CHAPTER 2

CHAPTER 2

protected from wind and sun and storm, and from the hungry eyes and ears of hawks and owls and predators from above.

Finally, on the shadowed forest floor, the real life of the forest exists in all its fecundity. Countless small creatures and insects live on and under the duff and leaf litter, helping to keep the forest clean. They tunnel into fallen trees and eat dead wood, they devour fallen leaves and dead plants on and under the ground. Fungi also dwell here in abundance—bracket and sulphur fungi, morrels and slime molds. And, of course, bacteria do their endless work here, helping to turn dead materials into the minerals needed by trees to grow, to find their place in the canopy above.

Walking beneath that canopy we look and listen—for the track of a raccoon or a mink, a deer or a gray fox; the twitching ears of a cottontail or the cluck of a chipmunk. If we are quiet and observant, we may find the tree hole of a chickadee or nuthatch; the hidey-home of a salamander; the soft spotted flank of a fawn.

In each season the woods is a different place. Late winter-early spring is the season of the "sugarbush," the rising of sweet sap in the silver maple trees, and the gathering and "boiling down" of it by eager syrup makers.

April and May bring the season of the wildflowers, as they seek their brief allotment of sunlight before the arrival of the canopy. Nothing is more beautiful and evanescent than a woodland wildflower. Look carefully in the Hormel forest and you may find the bright yellow bouquets of the marsh marigold in watery places where feet are always wet. Bend down close to see the delicate grace of spring beauty: hepatica, trout lily, wood anemone, or bloodroot. A bit later in spring, the fuzzy stems and soft leaves of wild ginger make their appearance, followed by the bold Jack-in-the-pulpit. Spring is also the season of migrating warblers, the achingly pure flute-song of the wood thrush, and the wafting music of the chorus frog.

Summer arrives in a rush—growth and activity and life in all its fullness. The canopy fills the sky, as millions of leaves use every sunlit moment to produce stores of food at unbelievable rates. Oxygen and water vapor escape in fantastic amounts through billions of microscopic holes in the leaves of each tree. Insects, birds, and mammals all are busy. There is, it seems, not a moment to lose in the warm and humid "lazy" days of summer.

Top: A cottontail rabbit pauses from feeding on clover.
Bottom: A Jack-in-the-pulpit rises from the earth.
Opposite: A young buck moves through the woods.

The throbbing evening song of tree crickets in late summer announces a change, and soon the woods begin to feel different. Things smell different as well. There is a tang in the air, a spice that increases with each passing day of falling leaves. Trails become noisy as squirrels rustle and scamper ever more frantically in their preparations for winter. The white-tailed bucks sport their full racks and scrape and rub in preparation for the rut.

CHAPTER 2

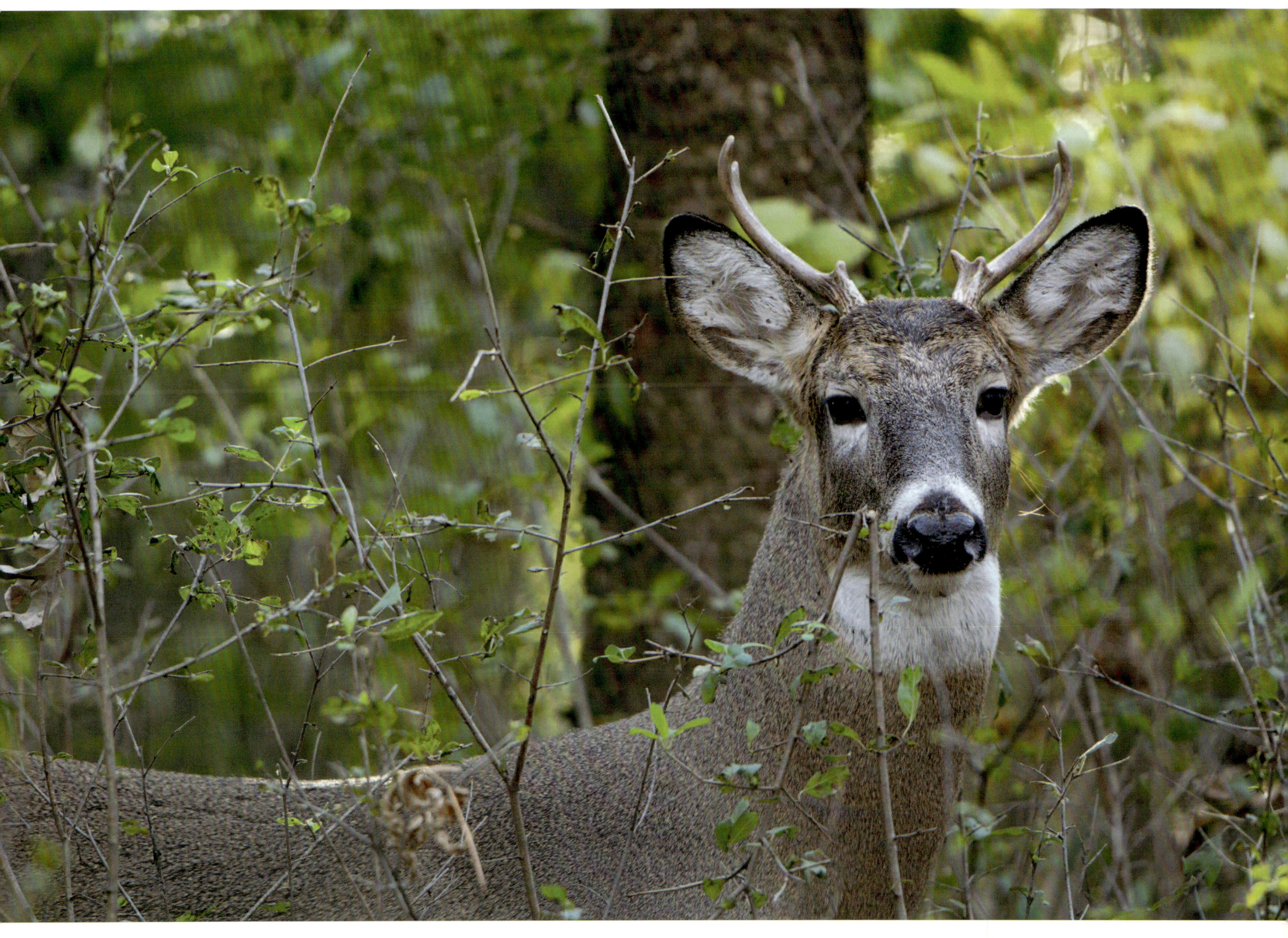

34

CHAPTER 2

CHAPTER 2

And with the arrival of winter, of long nights and short days, the grip of ice and snow brings a quiet and a calm not known for many months. It is a different world now. Life *feels* different. All is simplified. Time passes more slowly in the cold. Until finally, at some indeterminate point in March, the sap begins to rise in the maple trees once more, and the cycle of the forest begins again.

But one thing does not change with the passing seasons—the pure pleasure of a walk in the woods. "Whose woods these are I think I know," wrote Robert Frost. We know, too. They are Jay Hormel's and Roy Anderson's. But they really belong to all the succeeding generations of children and all who possess a child-like wonder. It is they for whom the woods were planted, and who enjoy them still.

So grab a walking stick and a trail map, and head for the green and shadowed spaces. Go and see the handiwork of a century of sunlight and wind and weather. Say a quiet thank you to Jay and Roy, if you think of it. Go for a walk in the woods.

The morning sun casts shadows of aspens onto fresh snow.
Opposite: The first leaves of fall rest on a forest trail.

CHAPTER 2

The north branch of Dobbins Creek flows through the forest.

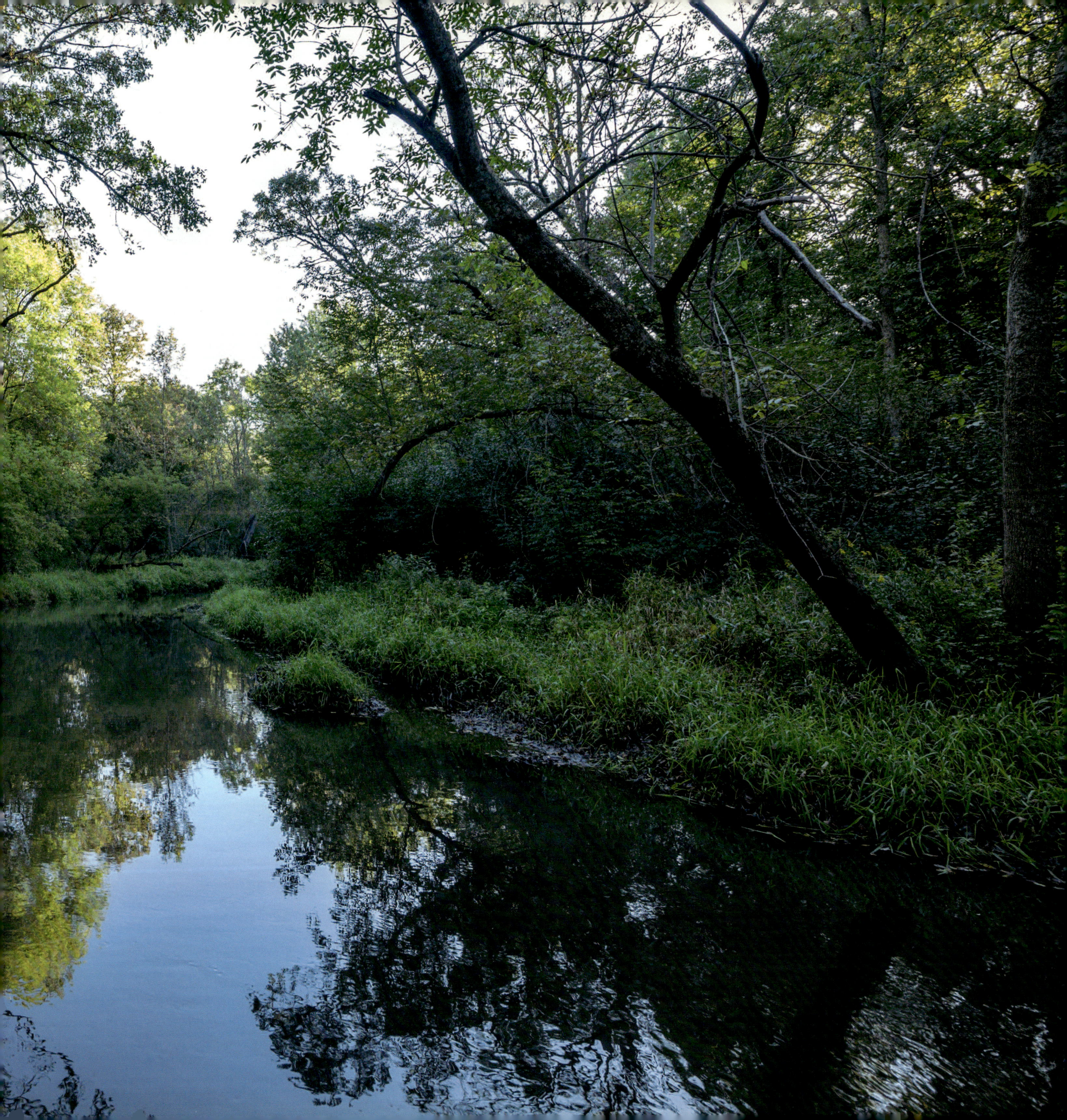

CHAPTER 2

An American woodcock sits in camouflage amongst the vegetation.

CHAPTER 2

From a nesting cavity, a male pileated woodpecker calls for his mate.

CHAPTER 2

Fungi grow on a dead tree trunk.

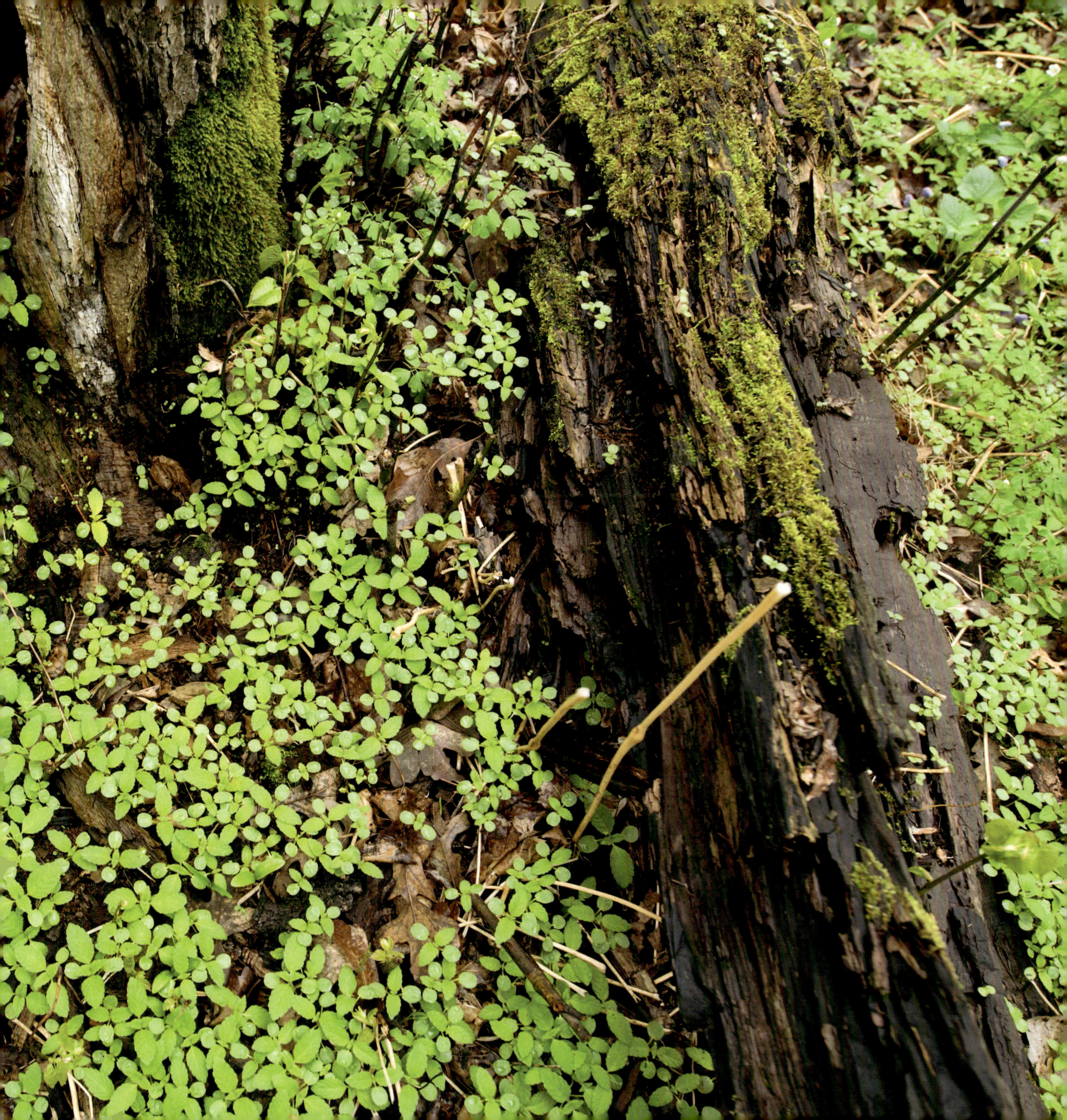

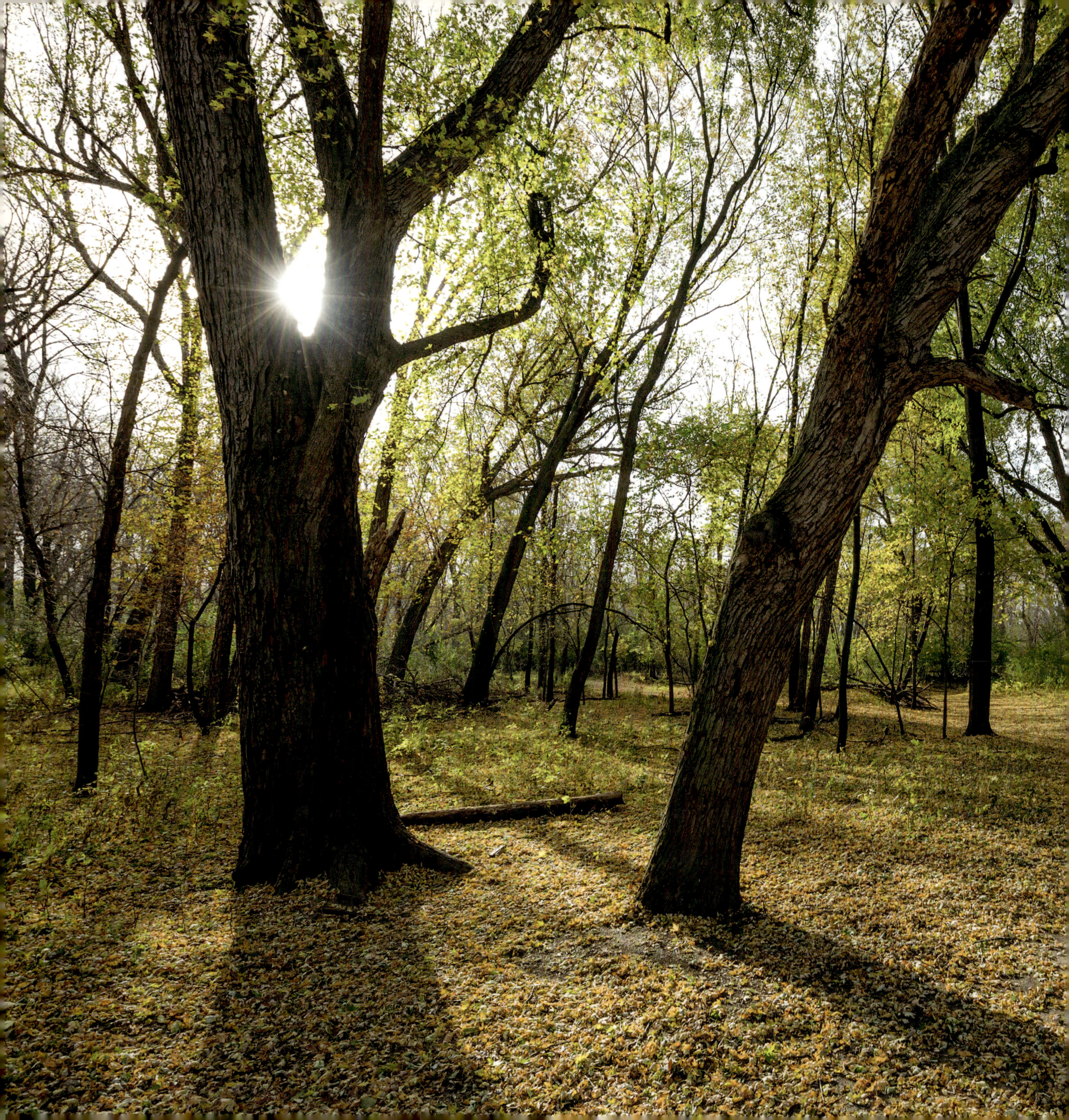

CHAPTER 2

Top: Northern flicker
Middle: Rose-breasted grosbeak
Bottom: Downy woodpecker
Opposite: Fallen leaves cover a hiking trail in October.

CHAPTER 2

A red squirrel appears and chatters noisily from its home in a tree cavity.

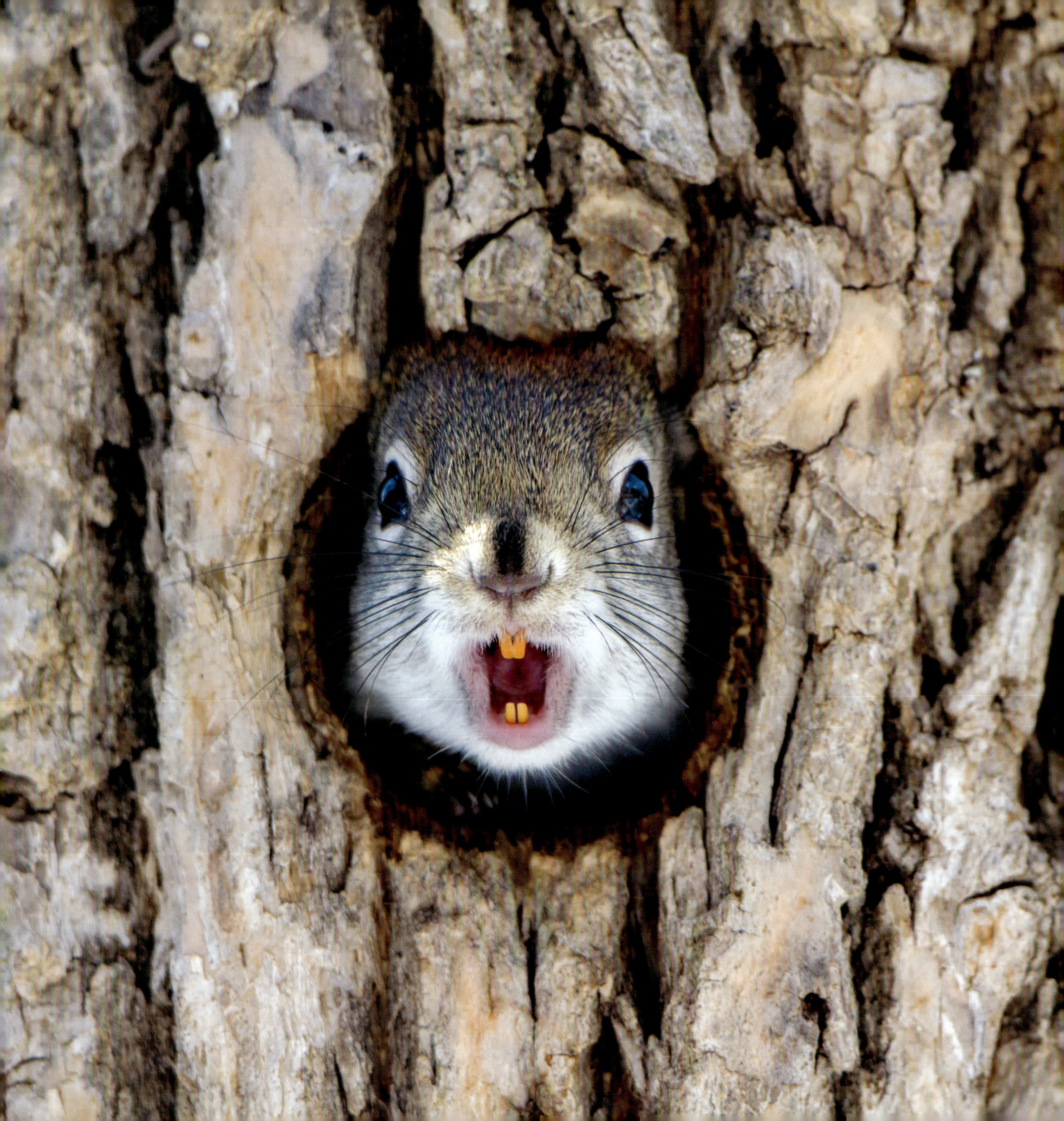

CHAPTER 2

Golden aspen trees glow against a blue sky.

CHAPTER 2

Aspens line the edge of the Big Bluestem Loop.

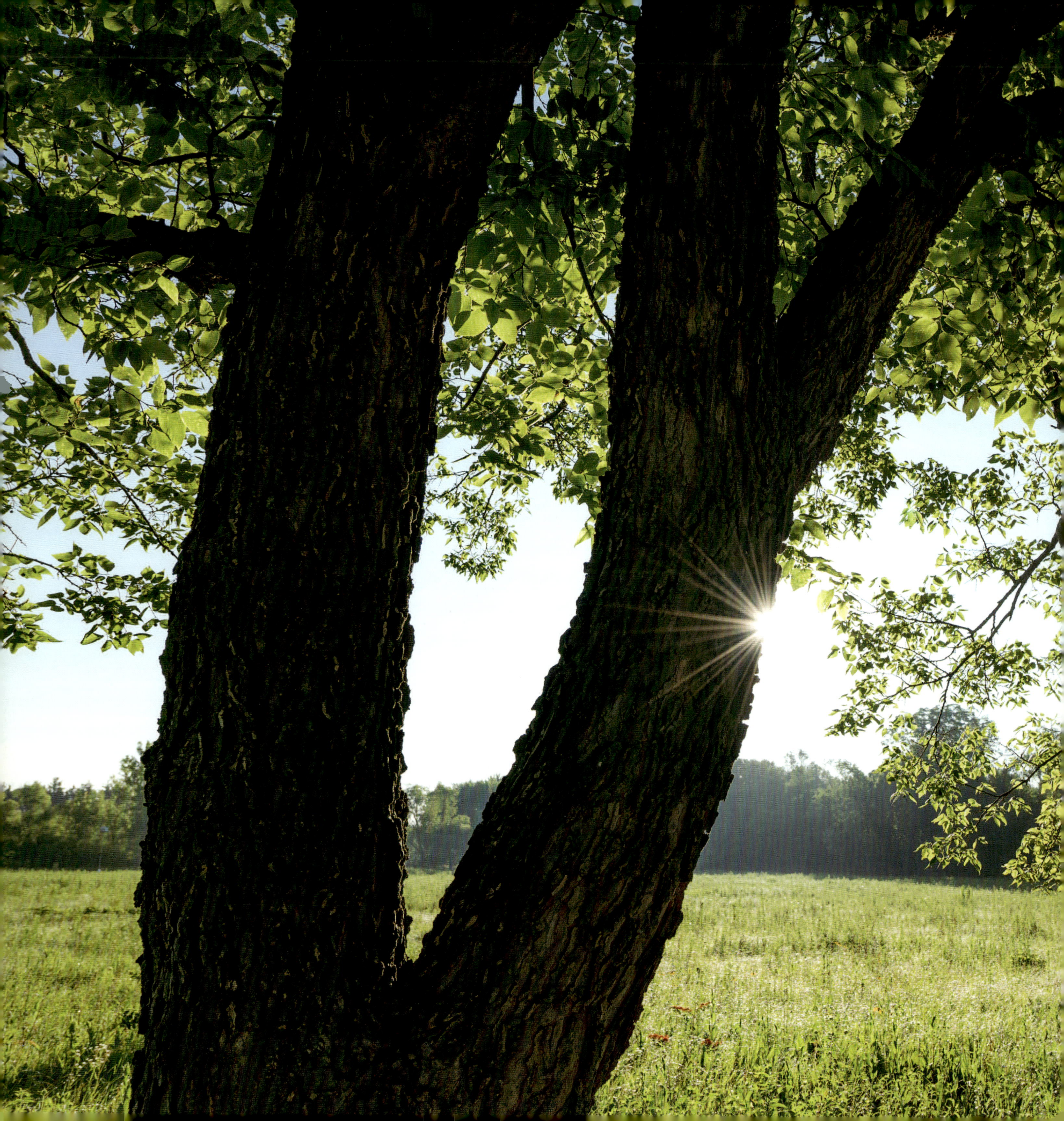

CHAPTER 2

Top: A cottontail rabbit cleans itself while keeping an ever watchful eye on its surroundings.

Bottom: A spotted fawn feeds on fresh clover.

Opposite: Sunbeams burst through the branches of a hackberry tree.

CHAPTER 2

In the spring, Virginia bluebells line the trails near the covered bridge.

CHAPTER 2

Marsh marigolds bloom on the Wetwoods Trail.

CHAPTER 2

Fallen leaves scatter under a grove of sugar maple trees.

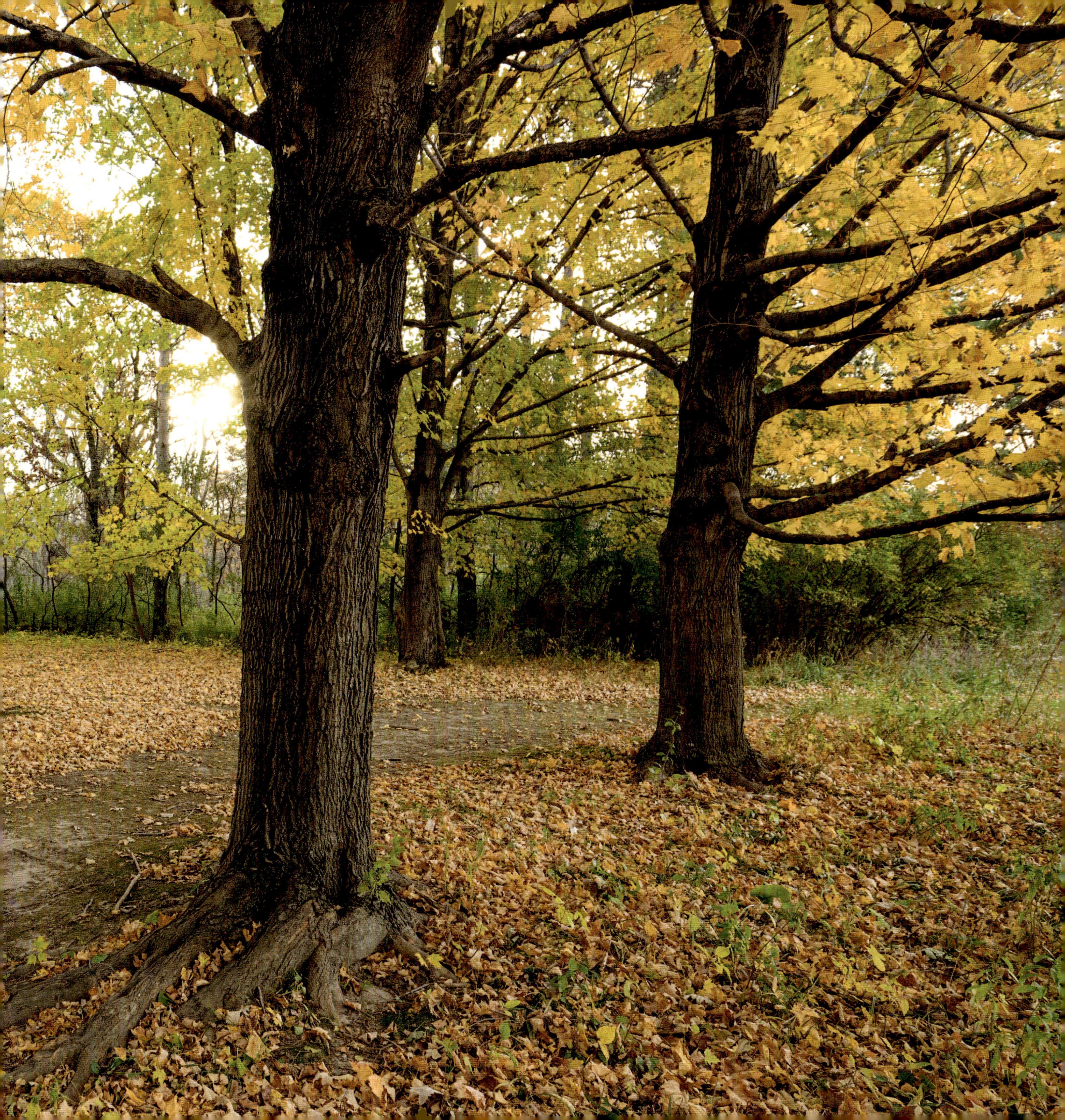

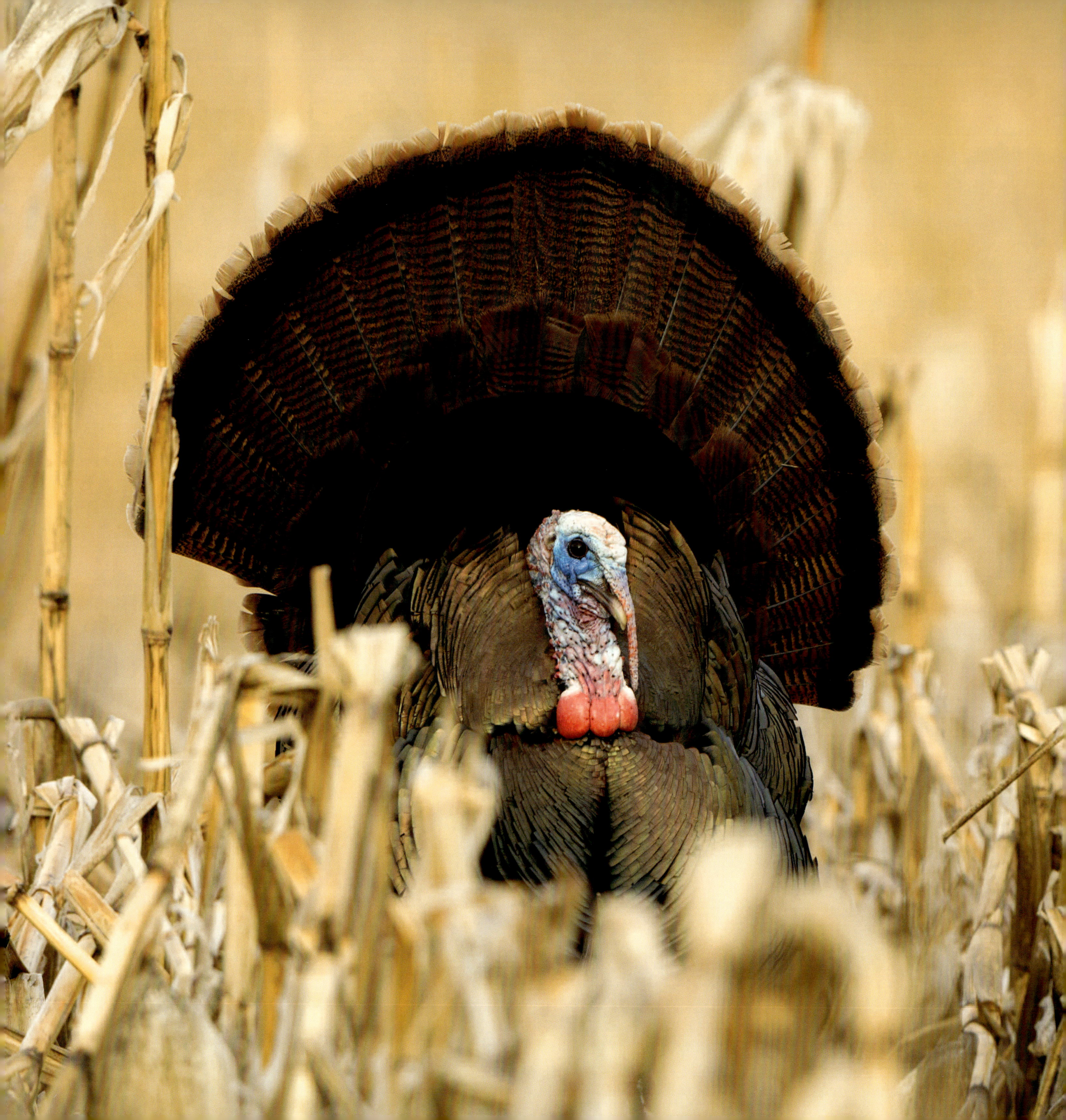

CHAPTER 2

A wild turkey displays in a cornfield.

CHAPTER 2

Top: Dark-eyed junco
Middle: American tree sparrow
Bottom: Blue jay
Opposite: Wearing a fresh blanket of snow, oak trees reach toward the sky.

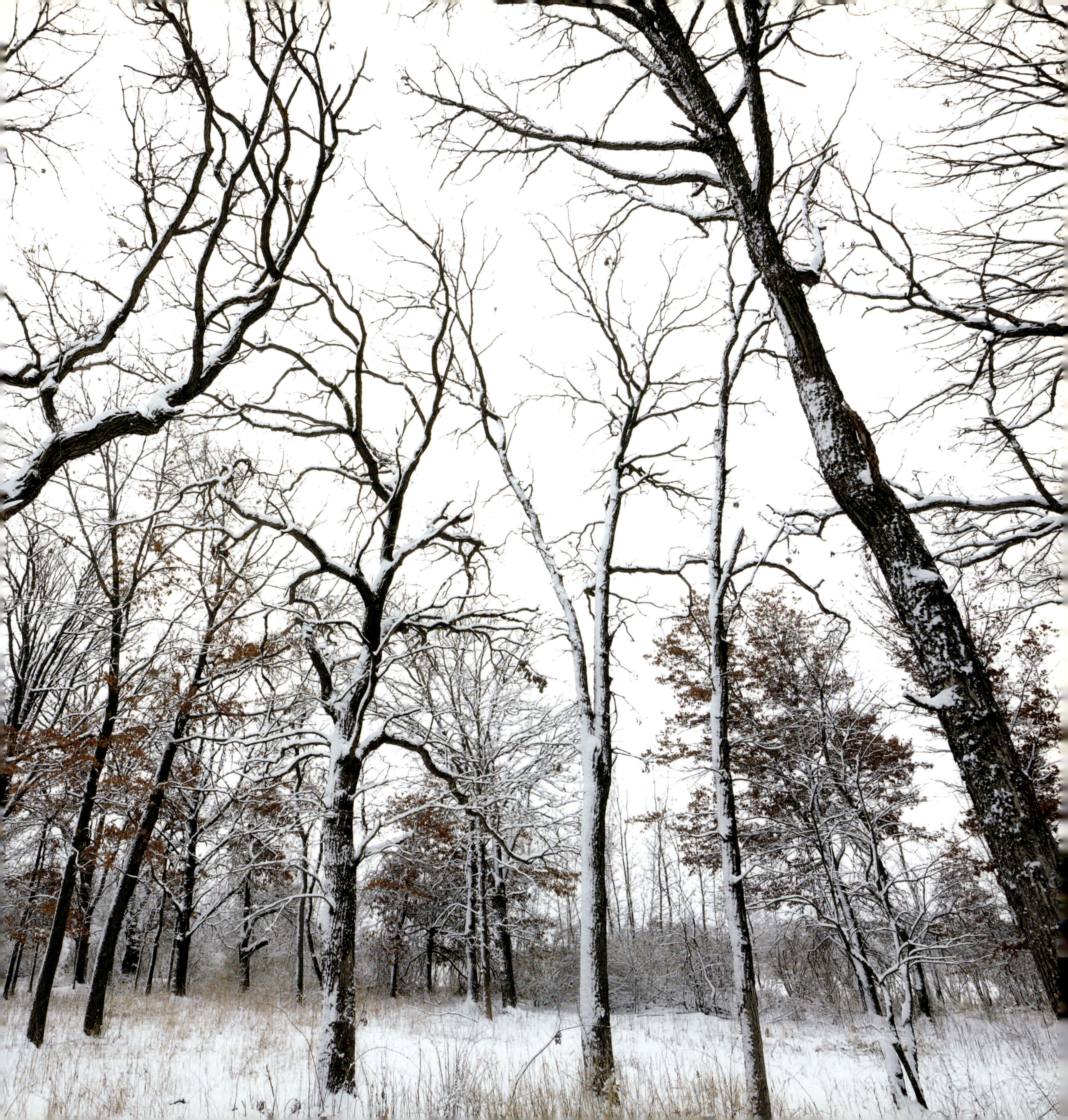

CHAPTER 2

Maple trees bask in the early morning sunlight.

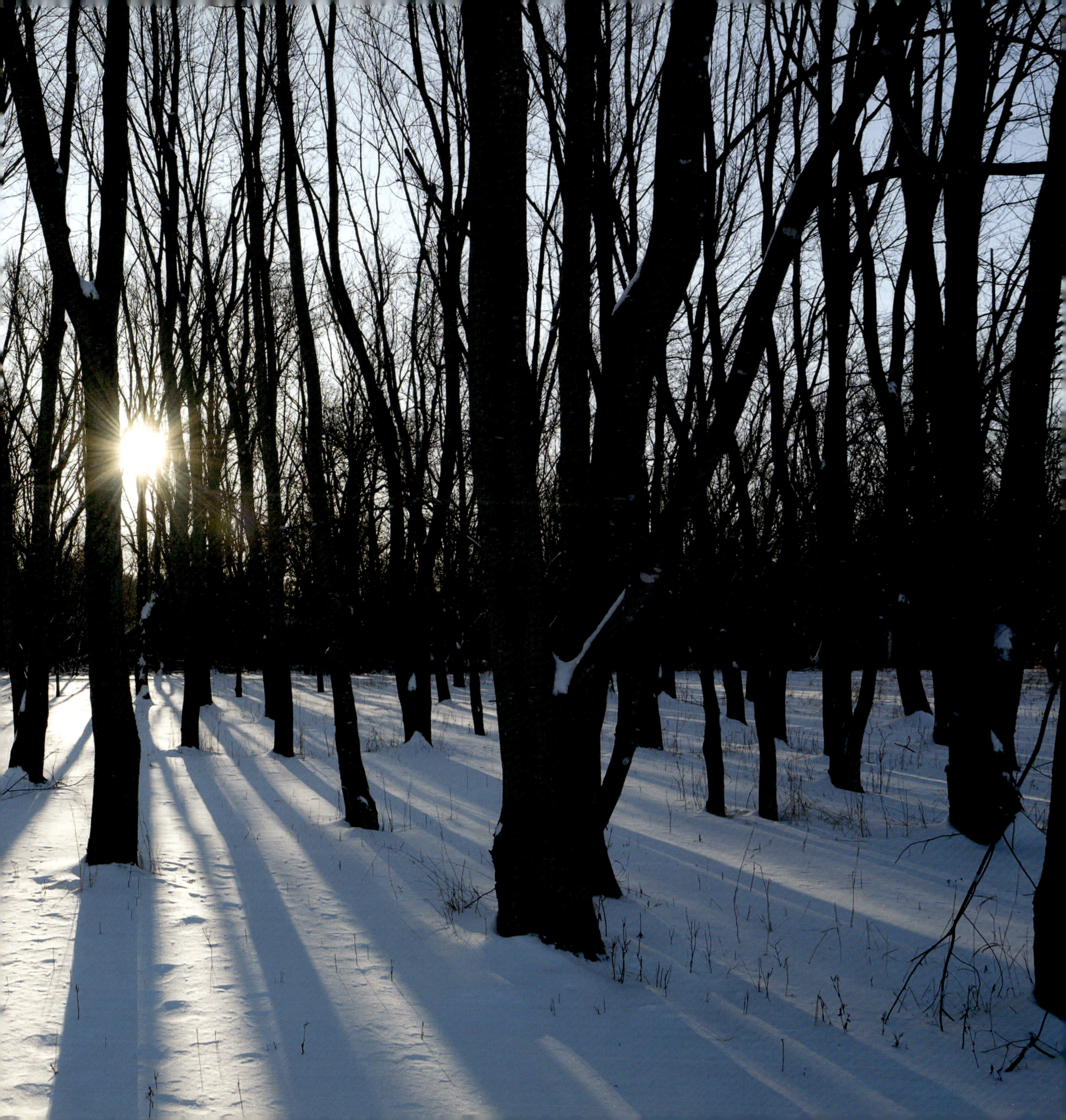

CHAPTER 2

A hermit thrush searches for food near the stepping stone bridge.

CHAPTER 2

A great crested flycatcher clings to a branch near the south pines.

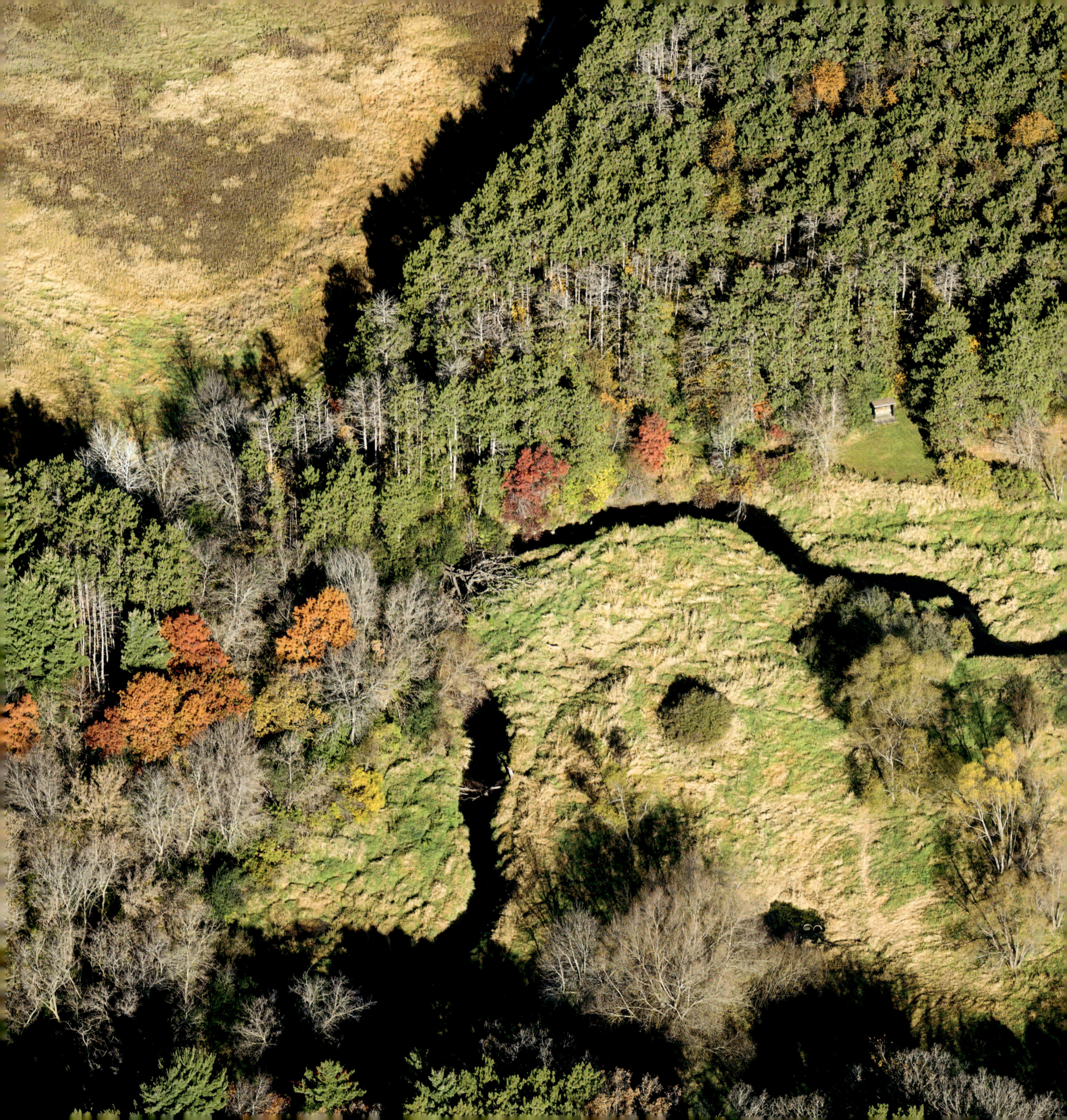

CHAPTER 2

The north branch of Dobbins Creek flows by a grove of red pines.

Black-eyed Susans stand tall on a foggy morning.

In all things of nature there is something of the marvelous.

—Aristotle

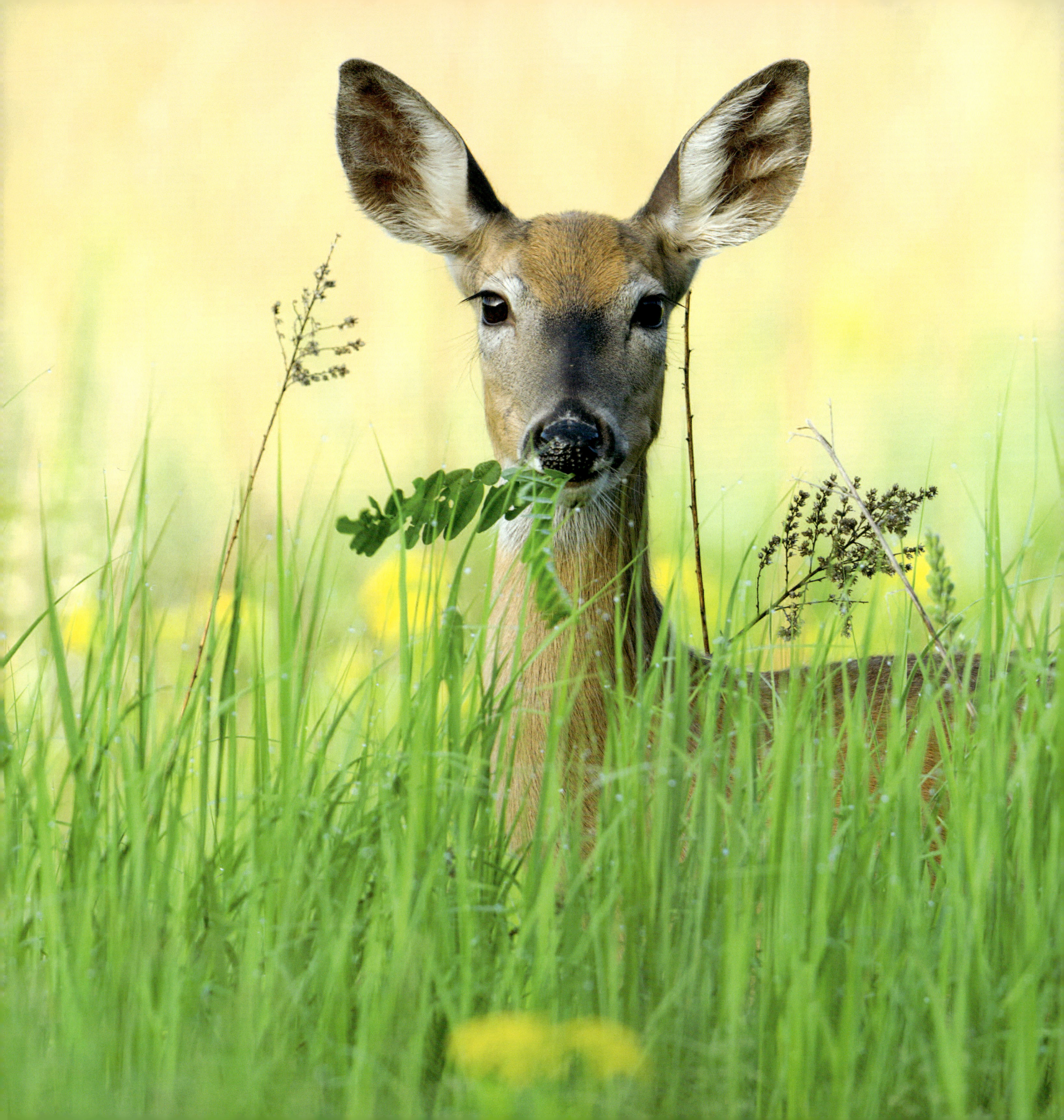

CHAPTER 3

A Patch Of Prairie—A Poem From the Past

It was prairie first, this stretch of land along a small creek in southern Minnesota. Or to be more precise, it was a portion of the American landscape known as the "oak openings" or "oak savanna," where the country transitioned from the forests of the east to the great sea of grasses out west.

This mid-continental prairie was one of the great natural heritages of our country, a web of interconnected life remarkable in both its vast sameness and its diversity. With the endless sky overhead and the endless earth below, the sameness stretched on seemingly forever to the eyes of the early settlers, sometimes terrifying in its expanse. Yet the diversity was also there for anyone to see . . . underfoot and overhead, in the almost limitless variety of plant, animal, and bird life: blazing star and pasque flower; bison, toad, snake, grasshopper, hawk. All were a part of the interwoven tapestry of life in the green, grassy sea.

For a sea it was, so much like an ocean that when the white settlers first began to traverse it they migrated in "ships"—prairie schooners, they were called—wheeled vessels topped by great shrouds of white canvas. In the oak openings, the settlers traveled under the tough, ubiquitous burr oaks, crowns and root systems so wide that they kept the trees comfortably spaced, allowing wagons to make their way easily beneath and between them. These sheltering oaks were armored with thick, impenetrable bark from the bottom of their trunks to the tips of their twigs, and thus protected from the fires that periodically swept the prairie. Meandering through the landscape, occasional streams and waterways provided flood plain habitat for other tree and plant species, and shelter for wildlife; and, with the arrival of settlers in the mid-1800s, the enhanced opportunity for farming.

So it was along Dobbins Creek, a small stream that still winds among some of the highest yielding farmland in Minnesota. The underlying bedrock, late Precambrian, is overlaid with topsoils of loess and till from the Wisconsin glacial period. It is distributed in this area as a mostly level plain without the deep canyons carved farther to the unglaciated east, nearer the Mississippi River. And it was upon this blanket of soil that the most noticeable feature of the landscape took shape—the quilted mosaic of grasses and forbs that gave the land its character. These plants, in their eons of growth and decomposition, immeasurably enriched the topsoil itself, until it became some of the finest on the planet.

Today the landscape of the Hormel Nature Center is still partially prairie, with scenes that provide a visitor just a hint of what this part of the world might have looked like prior to European settlement in the 1850s. A true prairie, of course, is vast—thus the metaphor of the sea. But today, with less than one percent of America's original prairie remaining, it is a rare blessing to get a glimpse, to be granted just a taste of what it may have once been like. Eighteen million acres of tallgrass prairie

A monarch butterfly feeds on rough blazing star.

Opposite: A white-tailed doe enjoys the fresh prairie vegetation.

CHAPTER 3

once graced the landscape of Minnesota. Today it is difficult to find a spot of prairie on which to place your foot. Beside Dobbins Creek, the bison and elk graze no more, and the audacious, booming dance of the prairie chicken is no longer heard—but the center is committed to an ambitious project of maintaining and re-establishing some last vestiges of this once dominant American land form.

Beginning in about 1978, the first small area was planted with grasses—mostly big bluestem and Indian grass—brought in from the Nebraska prairies to the southwest. Later, a variety of wildflower seeds were added to the mix. Since those earliest efforts, and after the arrival of Larry Dolphin as director/naturalist, the emphasis in subsequent plantings and reclamation efforts has been to try to replicate as nearly as possible the sort of prairie that was described in the earliest survey notes of 1854. Local nurseries and prairie seed sources are now used, and attempts are continuing to intersperse the grasses with the once common burr oaks. The oaks, it turns out, are difficult to get started. But once started, they are equally tough to kill, the secret of their predominance on the historic prairies.

The prairie of the Hormel Nature Center is now a remnant and a reminder, a fragmented patchwork quilt of the once awe-inspiring American ocean of grasses and flowers. Each prairie area provides invaluable habitat for species that in many cases are struggling to hold on in 21st-century America. It is now, of course, an America of interstate highways, cities and towns, parking lots, suburbs, subdivisions, and fencerow-to-fencerow plowing and planting, bearing scant resemblance to the land the pioneers of the 19th century found here.

Today each section of the Hormel prairie is looped by a trail—West Prairie Loop, Prairie Garden Loop, Lone Oak Loop, East Prairie Loop, Restored Prairie Loop, Tower Loop, Big Bluestem Loop—giving visitors a chance to walk a bit of prairie as our homesteading ancestors once did. Some areas are so luxuriously covered in tall grasses that a rider on horseback can barely be seen, just as in days of yore. Larry Dolphin has called the feeling the "prairie mystique," something hard to define, but easy to appreciate. Wandering a trail, one has the opportunity to meet the dickcissel, bobolink, savannah sparrow, or song sparrow. You may catch the flutter of the grasshopper or clay-colored sparrow; or perhaps hear the warbling of an eastern or western meadowlark. These opportunities are increasingly rare in Minnesota, because the habitat that supports such birds is rare. The voles, shrews, and white-footed mice, though perhaps unseen in the carpet of grasses, are here as well, once more a part of the world their kind has always known. A monarch butterfly rests atop a wildflower—a jewel atop a jewel. And the coyote, the red fox, the white-tailed deer, all inhabit their own place in this grassy ecosystem.

Opposite: A dickcissel basks in the morning sun from his prairie perch.

Such a habitat relies on one force above all others to maintain its integrity, its hold upon the land. It is a force often feared, or tamed for our own purposes, but is an essential and historic ally of the prairie. That force is fire.

CHAPTER 3

CHAPTER 3

CHAPTER 3

Prairies depend upon fire for their existence. It is a cycle of catastrophe and rebirth, destruction and renewal, as old as the prairie itself. Because the root systems of prairie plants are not heated to an intolerable level, burning does not destroy grasslands, but instead regenerates and reinvigorates them, as it removes competing species.

In the mesic and savanna prairies of southern Minnesota, big bluestem and Indian grass were the dominant grasses. In the drier gradients, the little bluestem, porcupine grass, and sideoats grama predominated, while in the moist areas, switchgrass and prairie cordgrass would be common. Wildflowers with names like pasque flower and milkweed, lead plant and prairie onion, black-eyed Susan, goldenrod, silky and aromatic aster, white indigo, prairie smoke, coneflower and coreopsis, bottle gentian and oxeye sunflower and blazing star, and dozens more, all traditionally called the prairie home. To say their names now is like reciting a nearly forgotten poem, and to walk among them is a stroll through history. And all depend upon regular fire to maintain their birthright in the landscape.

A thick patch of black-eyed Susans grows just north of the Tower Loop.

Opposite: White wild indigo and spiderwort bloom in tandem in early June.

CHAPTER 3

Without fire, such areas would soon be overgrown by shrubs and trees. On the Hormel property, aspens and dogwoods, among others, maintain a fairly constant attempt at invasion, barbarians always at the gates. So fire, ancient ally of the prairie, is employed in a rotating cycle, a continuing series of controlled burns. Every three years or so, each area is burned individually, under strict safeguards. The burns occur in the spring—late March, early April—with great care given to the mating and nesting patterns of birds and other considerations. But always there is the knowledge that in the context of the prairie, and with today's careful management, the flames bring life more than death.

Prairie plantings occur in both the fall and the spring, with the ongoing goal of recreating a living landscape, a tapestry. And though it can never replace the complexity and integrity of what was lost, it can be a tie to the past as well as a vital part of the present and future for countless species that need a place to call home.

The story of the Hormel Nature Center has always been tied to trees, with Jay C. Hormel's remembrance of his "lost grove" of childhood acting as a prime impetus for the original arboretum. Many of those early plantings tower into the sky today, and remain as a testament to the beauty and meaning of woods.

But in southern Minnesota, there is another tradition to honor as well. Before the plow and the disc, the combine and the corn picker, before the barbed wire fence and the cow pasture and the feedlot, there was once a sea of grass and wildflowers. There was once a prairie. And at the Hormel Nature Center, alongside Dobbins Creek and the beautiful woods, a little bit of it remains.

A bobolink serenades the prairie with its melodic song.

Opposite: The rising sun illuminates one of the many spider webs to be found among the prairie grasses.

CHAPTER 3

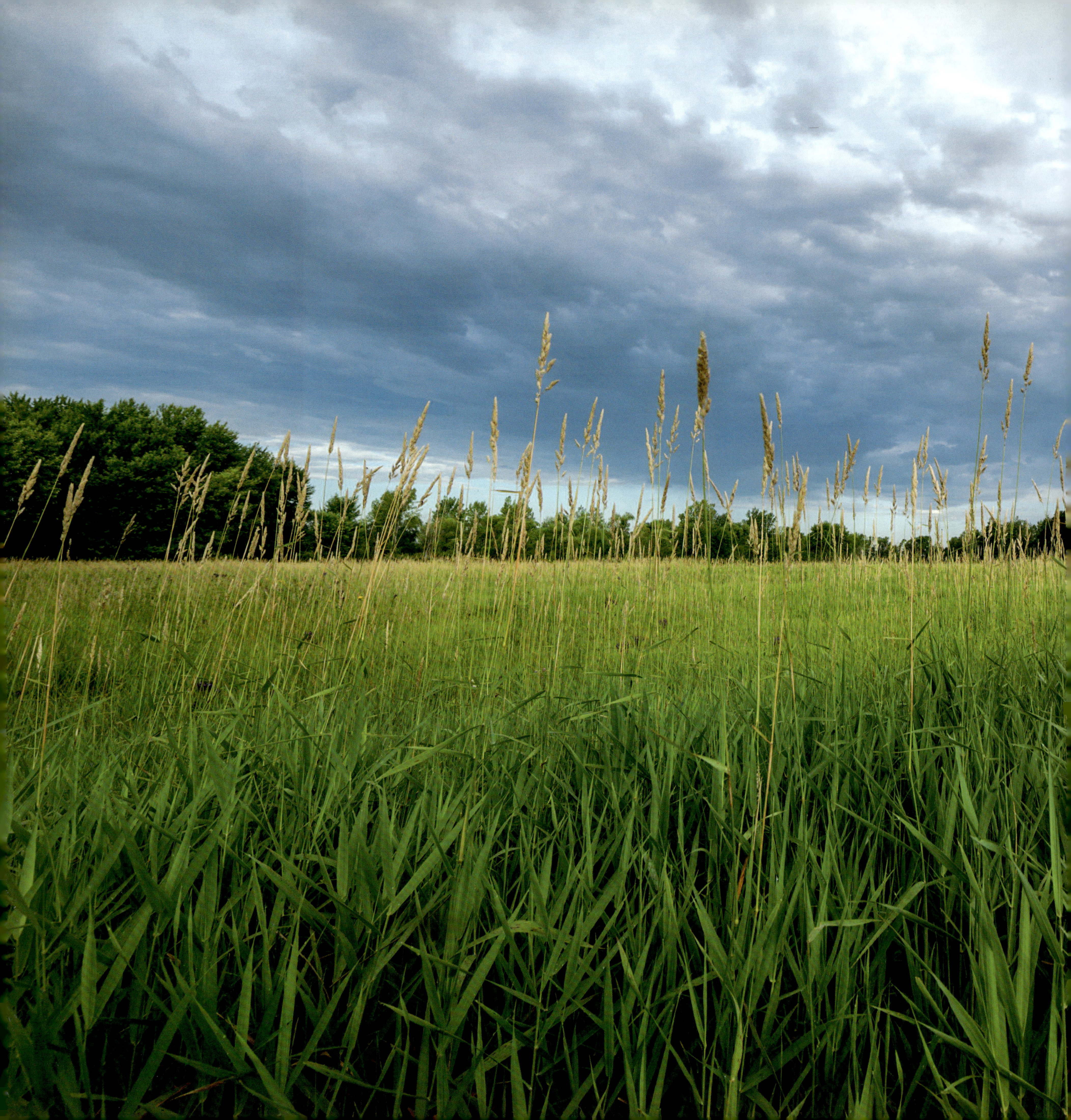

CHAPTER 3

Storm clouds approach the prairie in mid-July.

CHAPTER 3

A monarch caterpillar crawls across a milkweed leaf.

CHAPTER 3

A monarch butterfly spreads its wings on a cluster of black-eyed Susans.

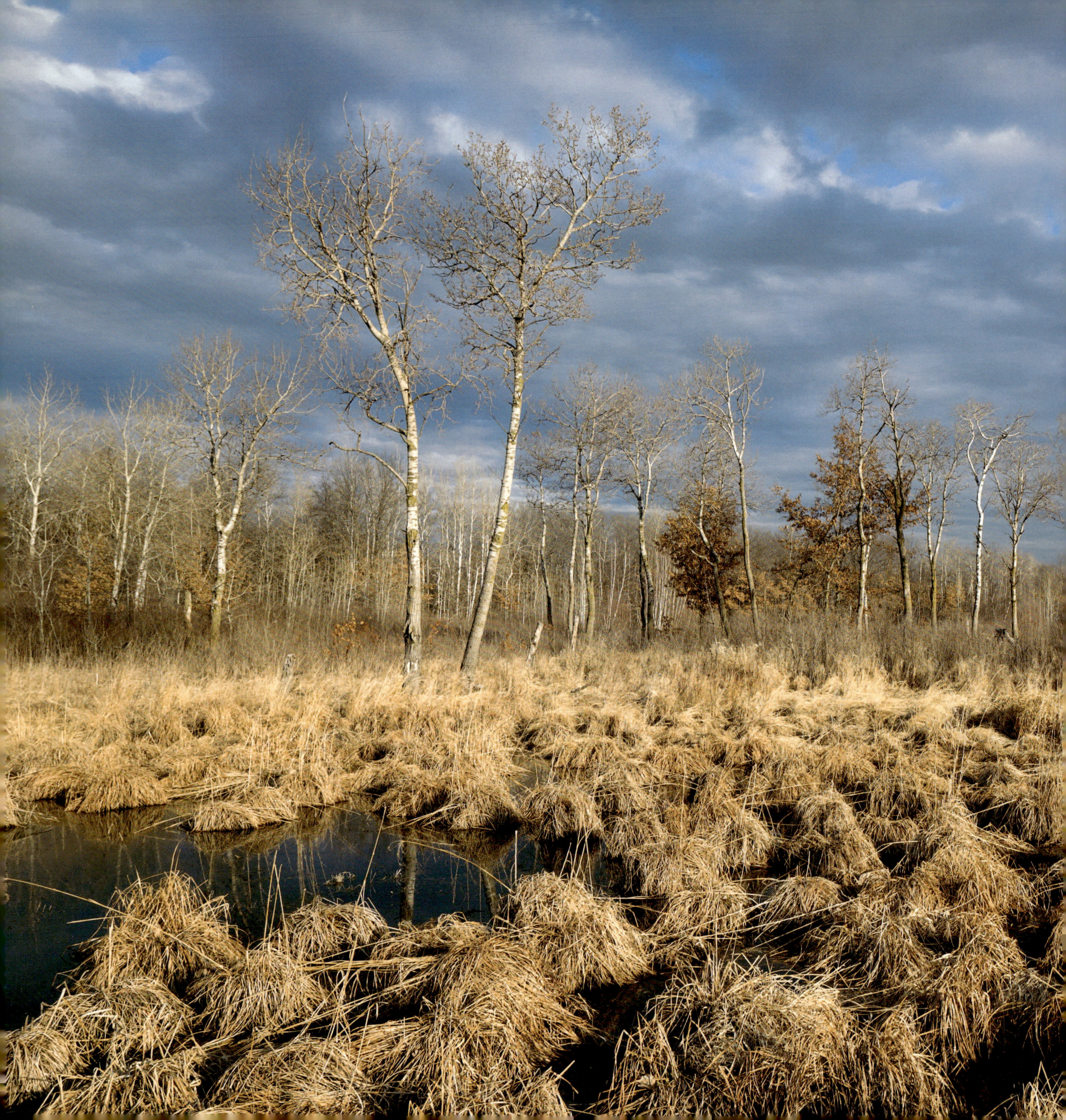

CHAPTER 3

Snowmelt creates a temporary wetland in the previous year's prairie grass.

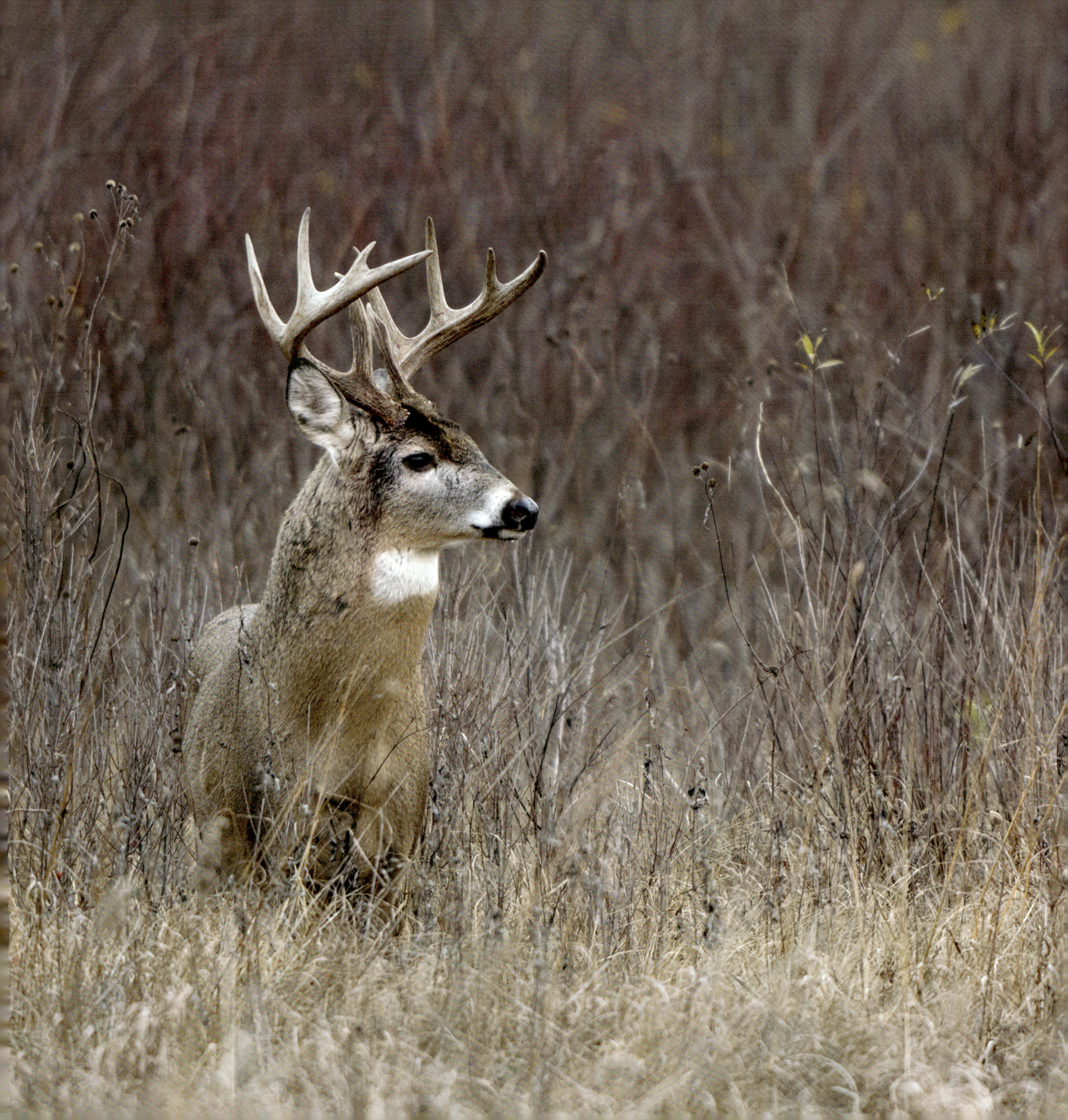

CHAPTER 3

A mature buck scans the prairie during the rut.

CHAPTER 3

The amber-colored prairie waves in the wind as clouds pass overhead.

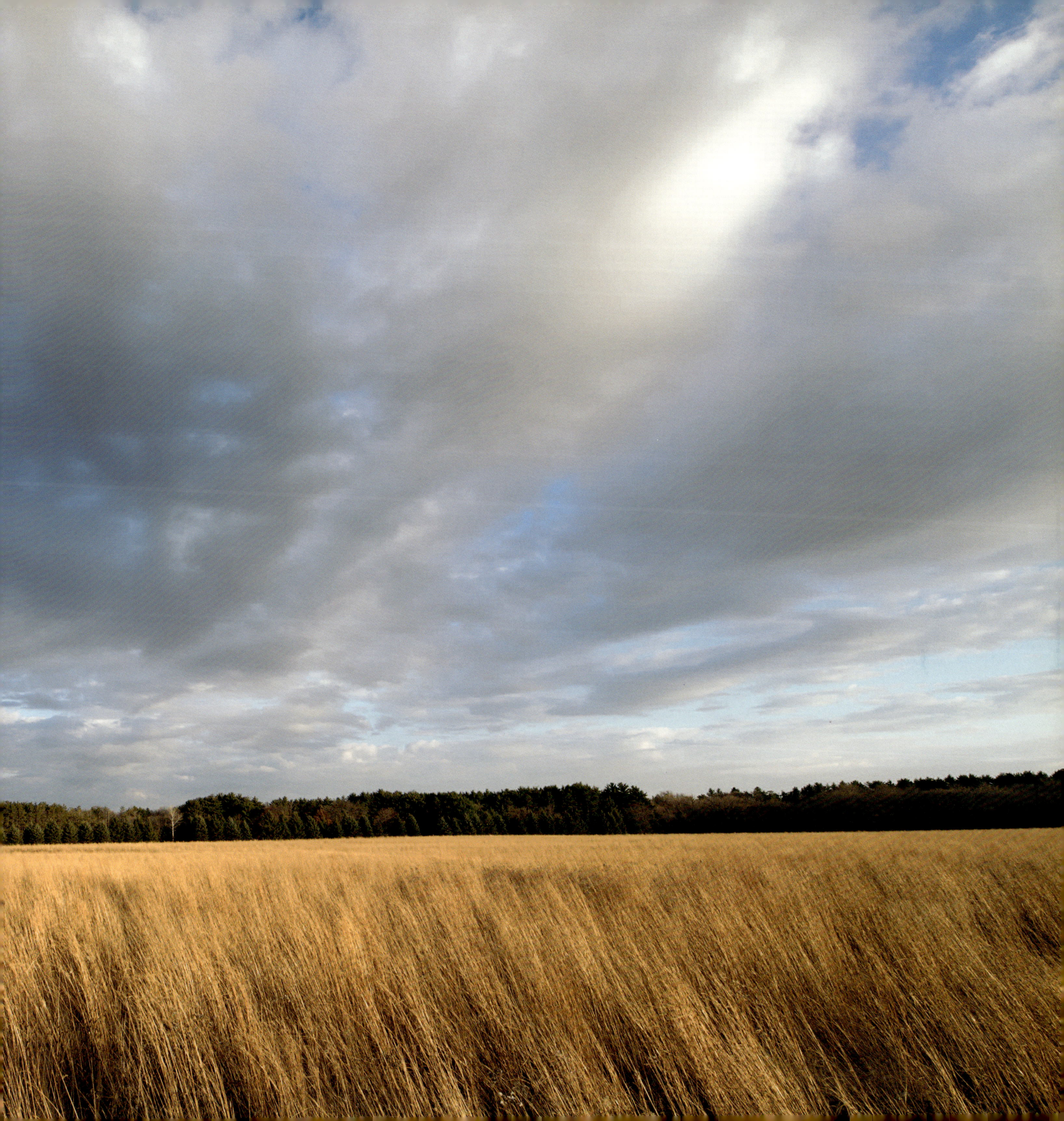

CHAPTER 3

A bald eagle feeds on a deer carcass until only the bones remain.

CHAPTER 3

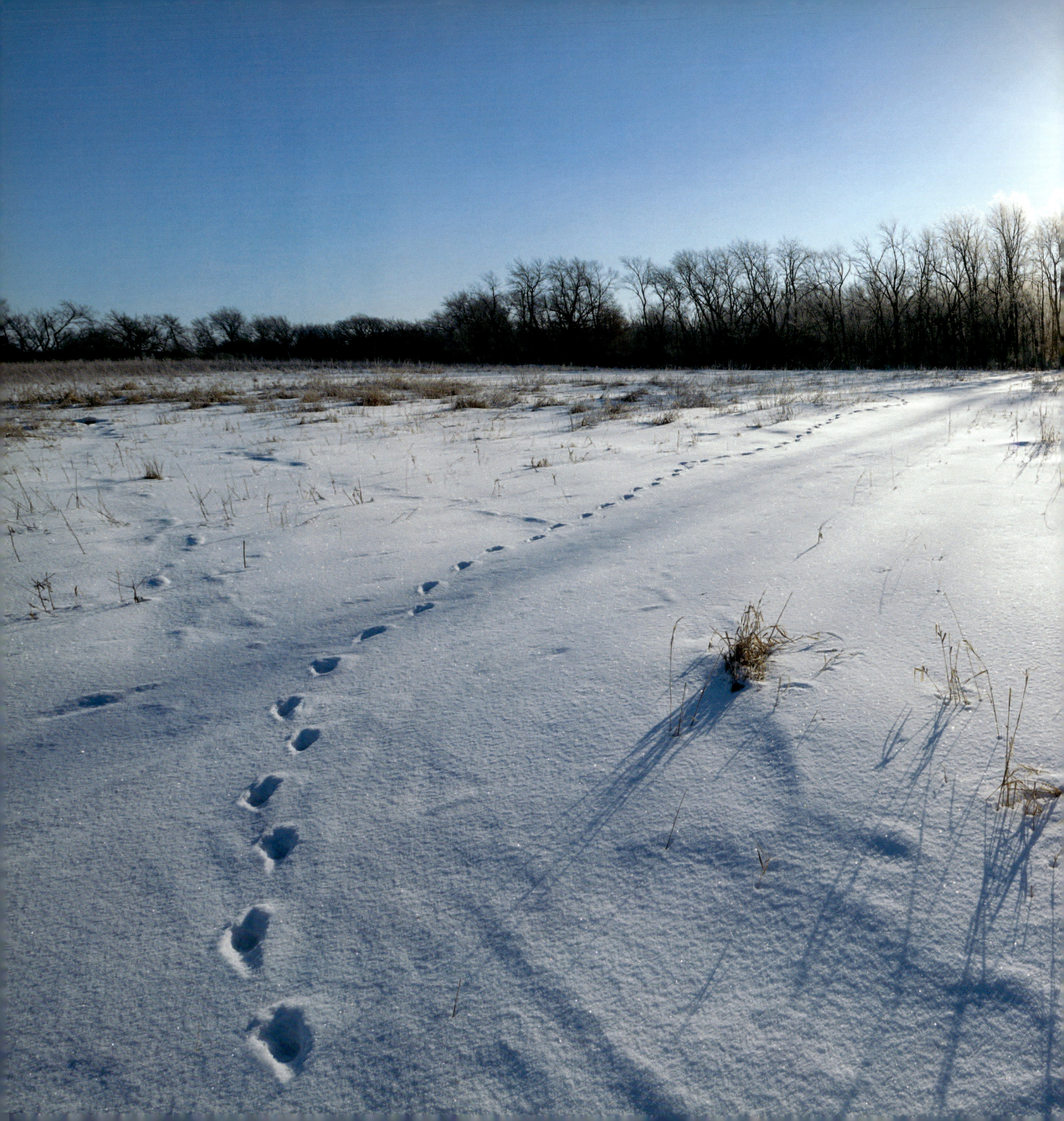

CHAPTER 3

*Fox tracks lead toward
the rising sun.*

CHAPTER 3

A young buck pauses in a frost-covered prairie.

CHAPTER 3

A ring-necked pheasant travels during a snowstorm.

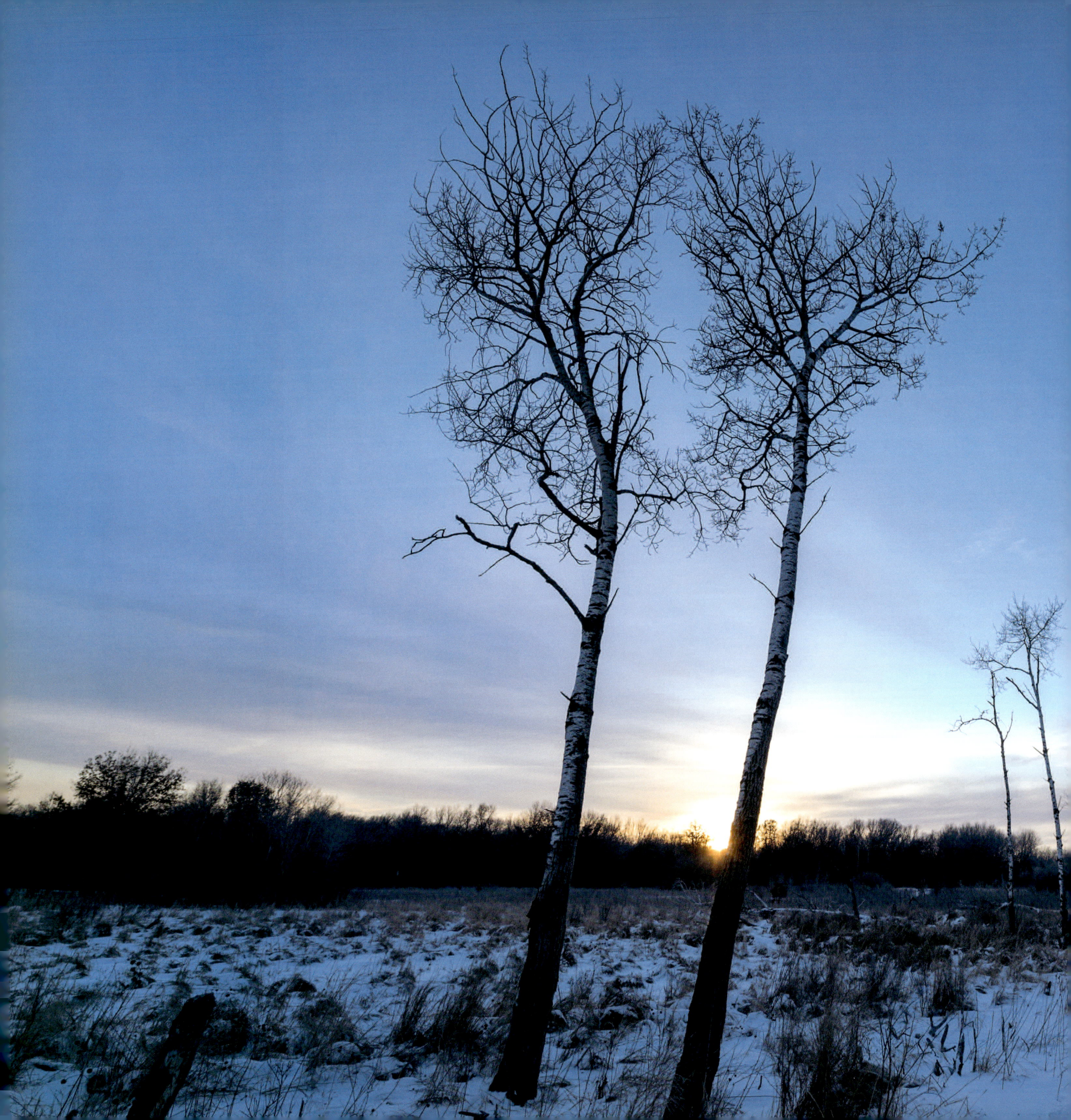

CHAPTER 3

The morning sun rises behind aspen trees.

CHAPTER 3

*Young oak trees grow on the
Prairie Garden Loop.*

CHAPTER 3

The windswept prairie meets the forest, with the observation tower nestled in the background.

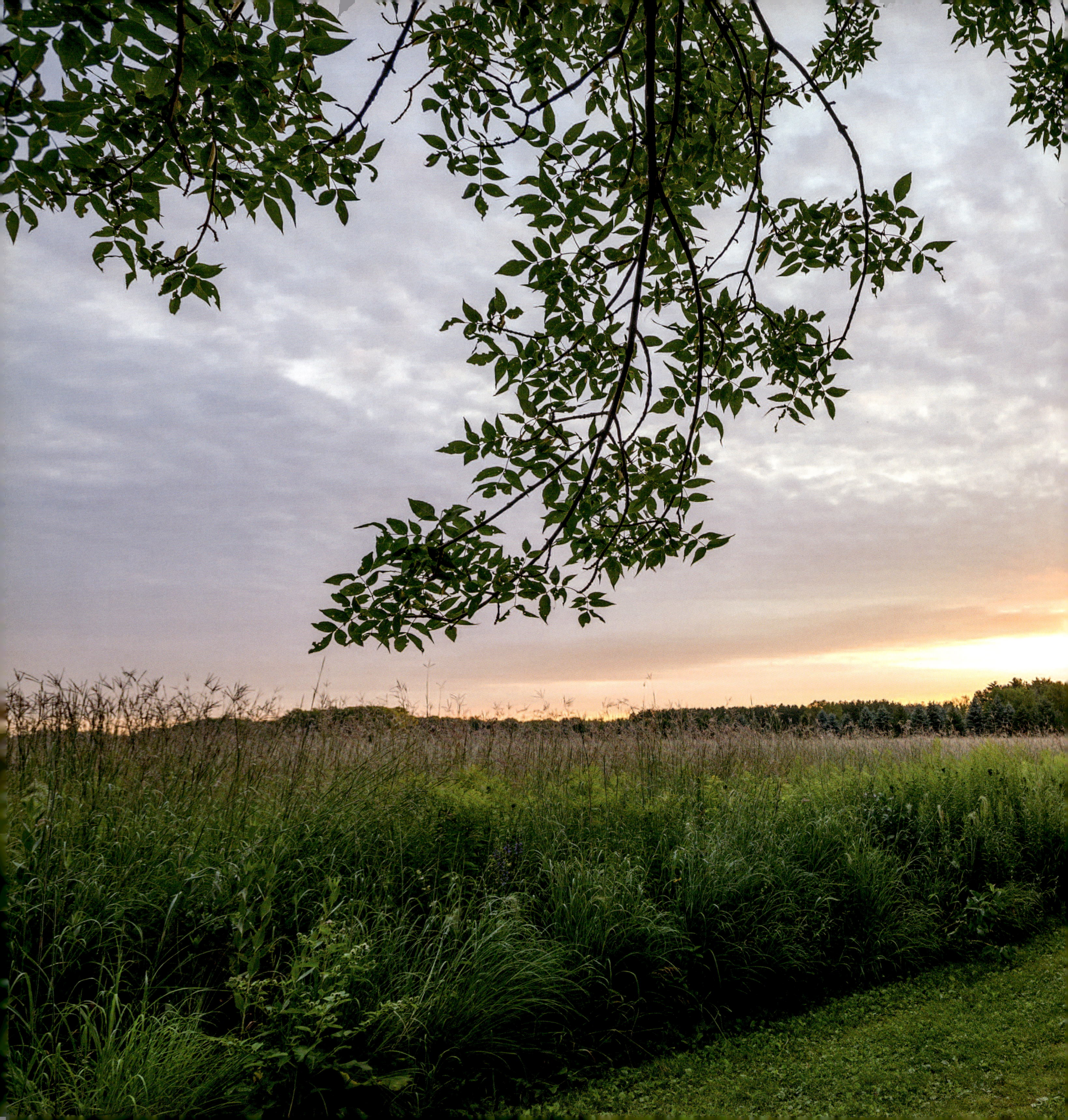

CHAPTER 3

A hiking trail divides the prairie and forest, creating a boundary between tall grasses and hardwood trees.

CHAPTER 3

A song sparrow sings in the early morning sunlight.

Opposite: A female cowbird rests on great angelica, one of Minnesota's tallest wildflowers.

CHAPTER 3

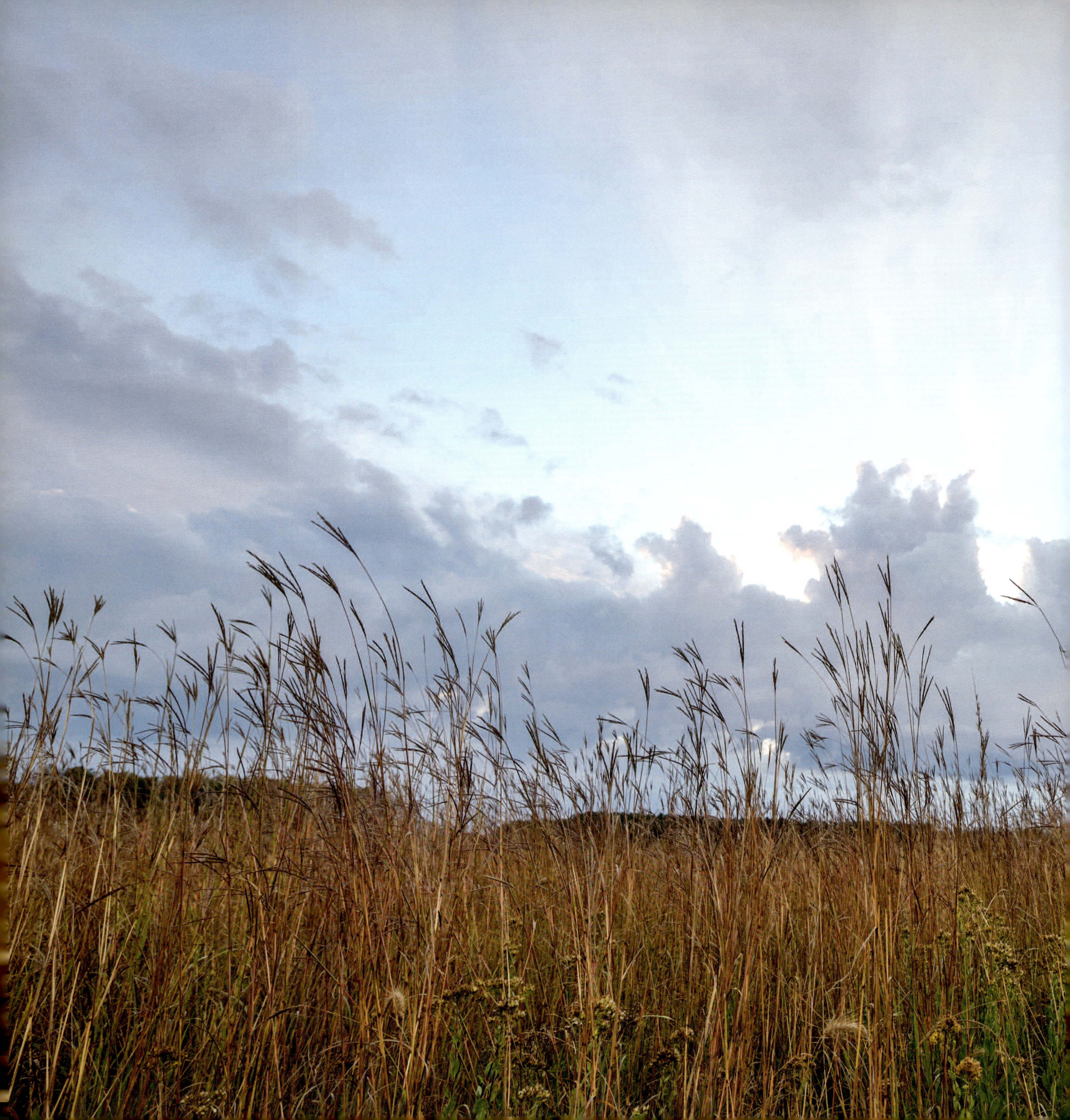

CHAPTER 3

Big bluestem stands tall against the rising sun.

CHAPTER 3

The flower of a compass plant and other prairie plants await a midsummer thunderstorm.

Opposite: Pale purple coneflowers, uncommon in the nature center, grow sparingly in the Prairie Garden Loop.

CHAPTER 3

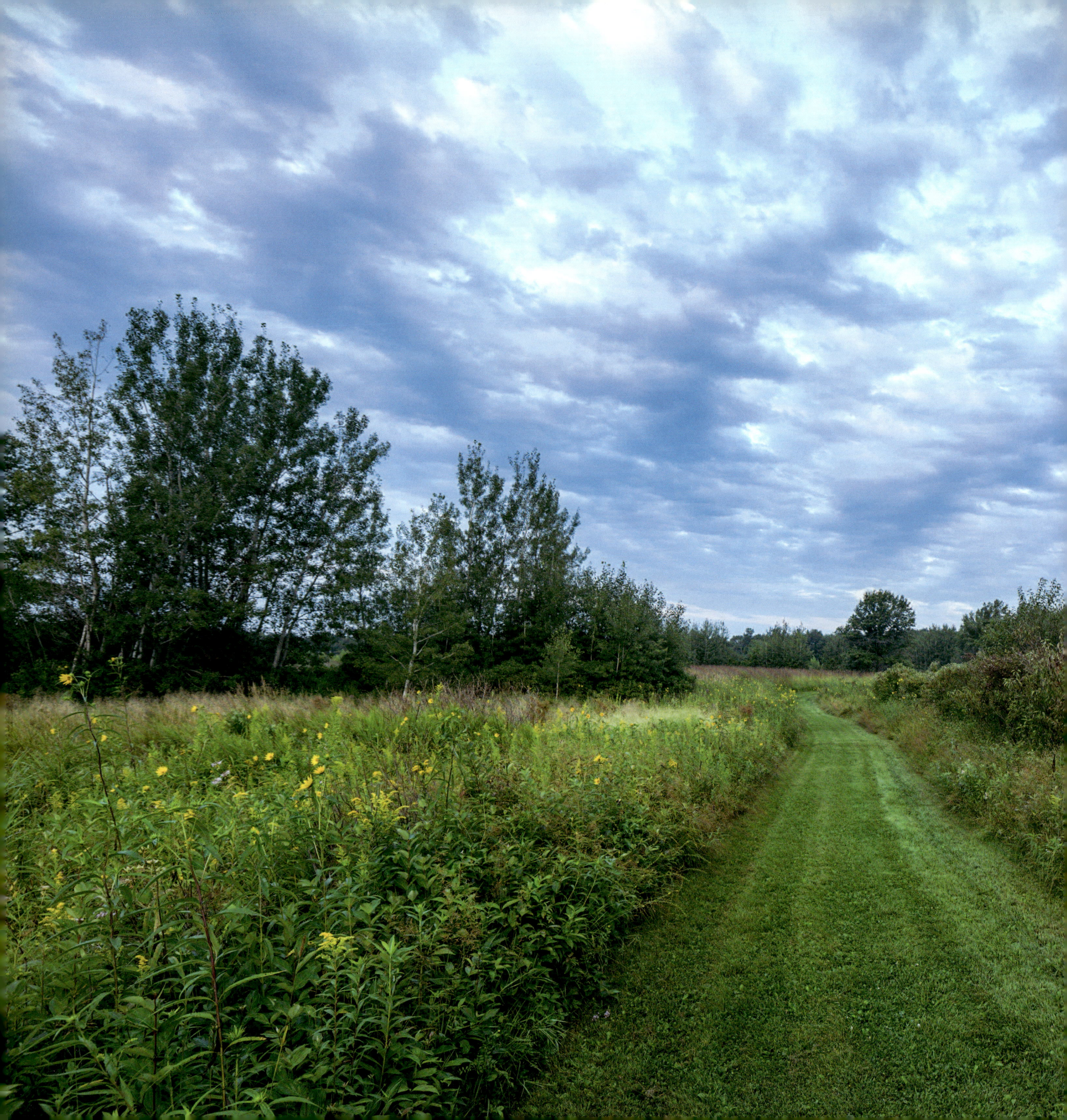

CHAPTER 3

A trail cuts through a lush prairie, filled with black-eyed Susans, bergamot, and goldenrod.

CHAPTER 3

CHAPTER 3

A coyote stands in a thick patch of dandelions.

CHAPTER 3

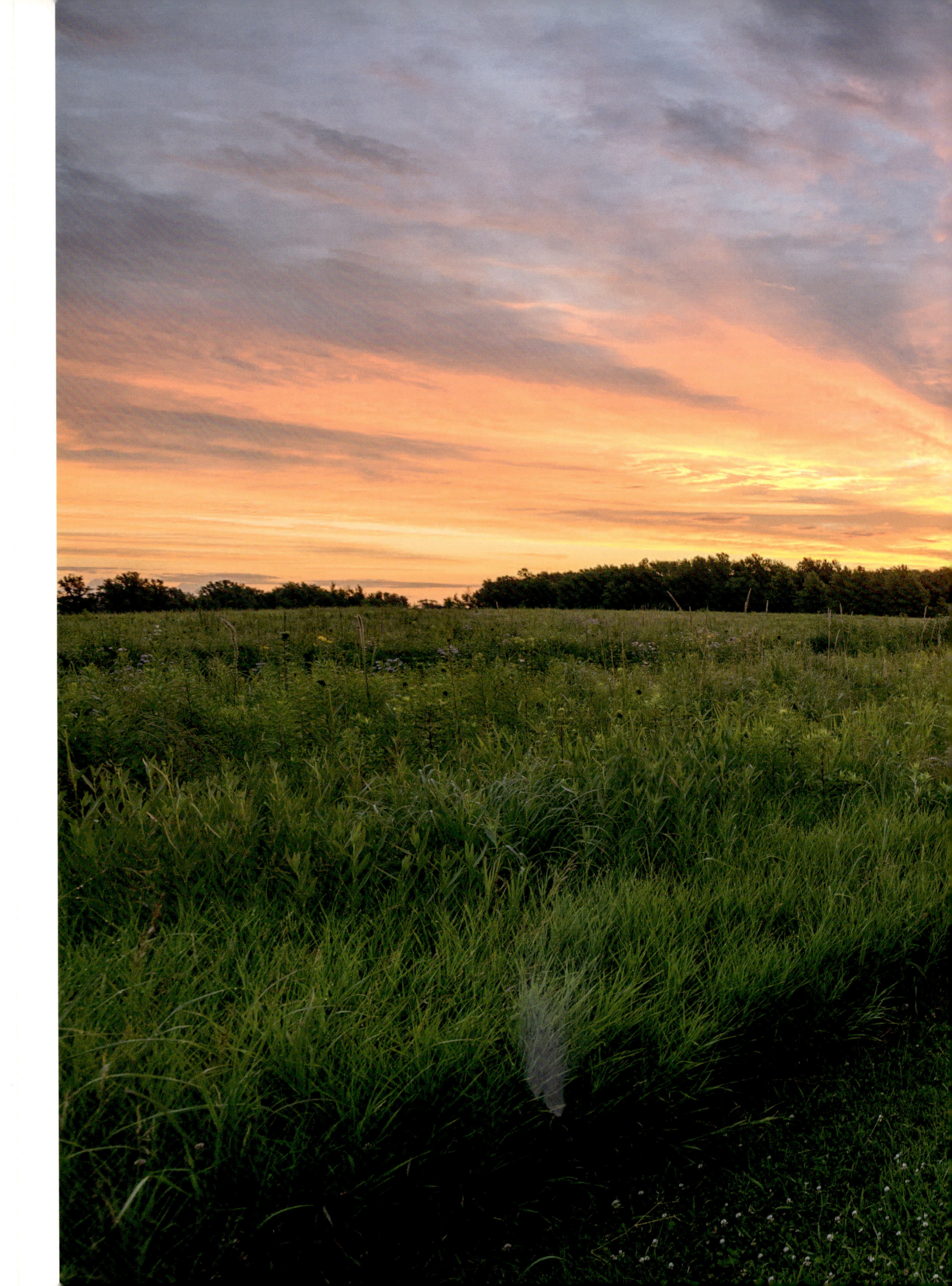

A sunrise over the prairie paints the sky as the earth awaits the sun's warmth.

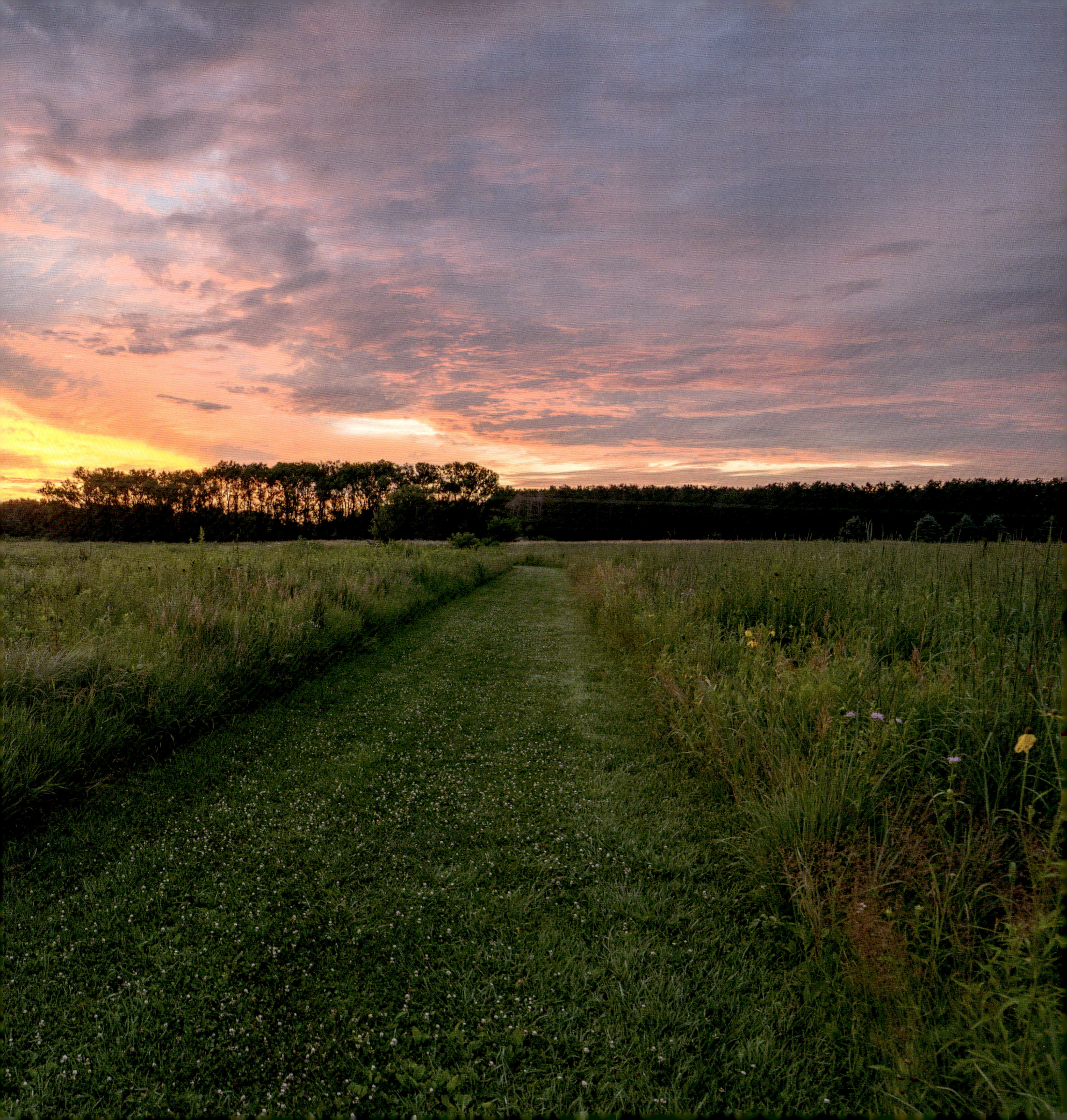

Painted turtles look for a way onto a log to soak in the warmth and energy of the sun.

Water is the driving force of all nature.

—Leonardo da Vinci

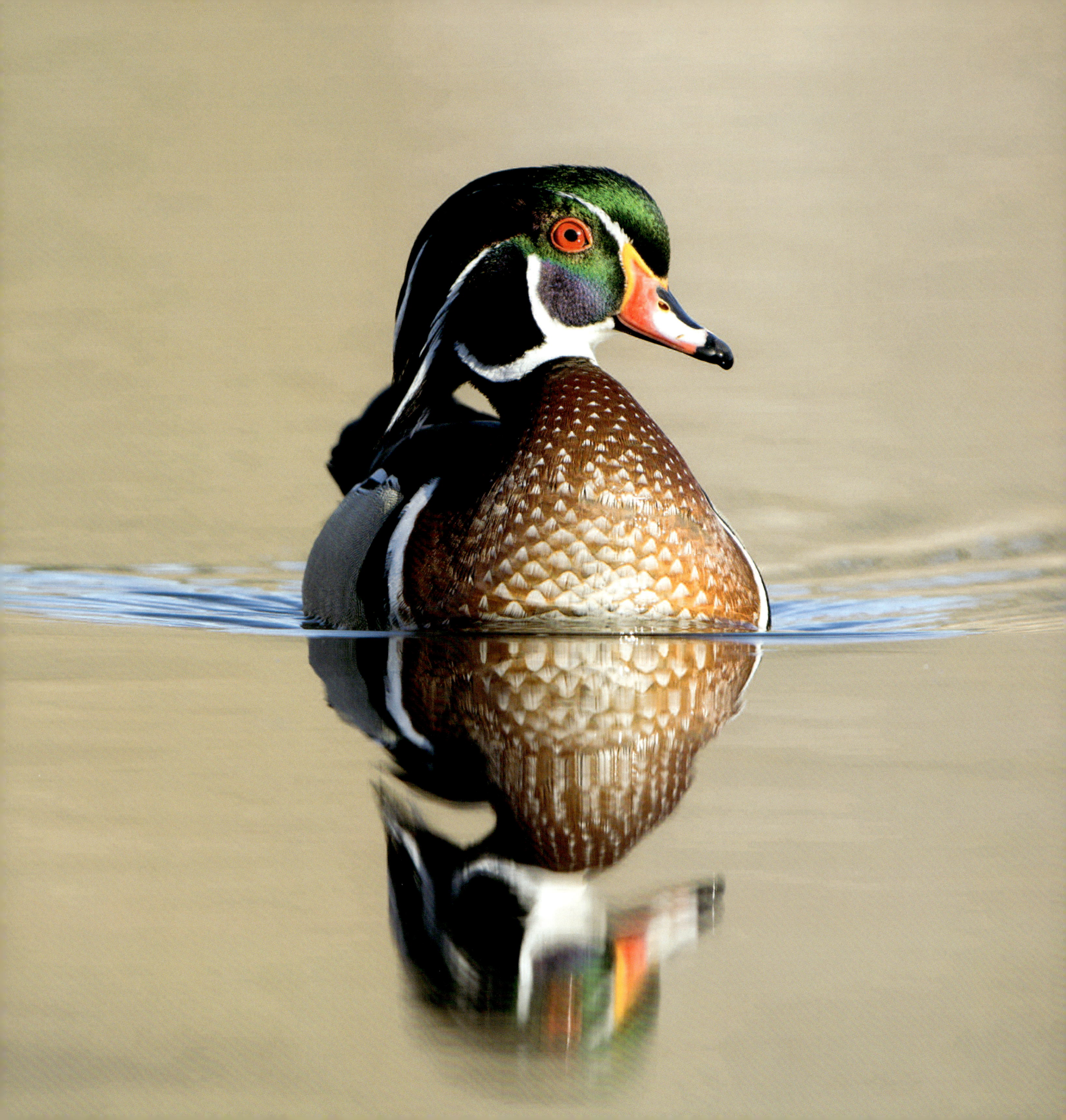

CHAPTER 4

A Pond on the Prairie

There is something about a pond. Or a lake or a sea or any reflective body of water. It doesn't have to be big; it doesn't have to be deep. It doesn't have to be a long way to the far shore. It needn't be broad enough for a sailboat or a yacht or a cruise ship. Maybe a Huck Finn stick raft. Or a canoe. And it should have dragonflies and turtles and frogs. A few cattails, maybe. Other than that, the requirements are minimal.

What a pond does have to do is reflect the sun, the moon, and the stars, and the thoughts of those who gaze upon it. It needs to stir the imagination, even if only in the most humble and unpretentious of ways. It is a healthy thing for body, mind, and soul to rest on a muddy bank like a damselfly or a leopard frog. To dip a paddle and watch the ripples spread. To simply . . . be. Countless generations of human beings have known and understood that it is good to be near the water.

"A lake is a landscape's most beautiful and expressive feature," wrote Henry David Thoreau. "It is Earth's eye, looking into which the beholder measures the depth of his own nature." Thoreau could have been talking about a pond as well as a lake. And in fact he was: for it was of Walden Pond, now canonized and sanctified among all small bodies of water, that he spoke.

Unfortunately, not all landscapes are blessed with ponds and lakes. Minnesota has far more than its fair share, but the prairie of Mower County is not lake country. After some years it became apparent that for a nature center, a pond was needed. And so in 1973, a pond was created. The fact that it was not formed by a glacier or by the finger of the Great Spirit, but was instead carved by shovels and earth-moving machines, could be imagined to detract just a bit from the underlying aesthetics. But the dragonflies don't seem to mind. And neither do the cattails nor the green frogs, the kingfishers nor the wood ducks, the green- or blue-winged teal, the painted turtles nor the snappers nor the Canada geese. All seem to agree that it is a fine pond indeed, and fulfills all the duties and obligations that a pond should meet.

Because the pond was excavated, a small "hill" of removed soil exists nearby. It is known, unofficially, as Turtle Hill, for it is here that the turtles of the pond create their nests in the spring to lay their eggs. Once again, it is not an "original" hill; but again, the turtles do not seem to mind. Each spring they heed the call to embark upon a journey nearly as old as the hills themselves, and appear quite content to take advantage of the good fortune that placed this small and earthy eminence near their home. The kingfisher, too, occasionally excavates his elbow-shaped, tunnel-nest in the sandy mound.

The vibrant colors of a wood duck reflect off the water's surface as it swims through the pond.

CHAPTER 4

Having the chance to observe the ancient nesting rites of turtles or kingfishers is only one of the benefits of having a pond. There are many more. To hear the bright "witchety-witchety-witchety" of the common yellowthroat, the bold "cong-ga-ree" of the red-winged blackbird from the cattails and the rising, comb-tooth song of the chorus frog, the soft muttering of the mallard, the gentle snoring of the leopard frog, the honk of the goose—all are an auditory treat, and all are notes of a natural and timeless music that soothes ears too often ringing or worn raw from the noise of traffic and machines and broadcasts. They are sounds that human beings have known from the dawn of time, and that should remain a part of the soundtrack of our lives.

To watch the twirling of the muskrat's tail and the spreading ripples from his wake as he goes about his rounds; to see a great blue heron standing like a statue, then stabbing his knife-like bill in a blur of speed at a small minnow or frog; to watch the swoop of the green heron, the long-legged walk of the water strider and the wild, chaotic motion of whirligig beetles; to observe the splitting of the dragonfly nymph's black armor, and the gradual and miraculous emerging of the green darner to dry its silvery wings in the sun—these are sights that human eyes evolved to see, as much as the track of the mink, the raccoon, or the deer, all left surreptitiously in the night. In the seeing of such things, we are reminded of our own roots and of the ancient call of watery places upon the human psyche. It is a past and a connection not so far away as we imagine, and the chance to rediscover it is invaluable.

A pond of less than an acre, only three- to four-feet deep, would seem too small to fulfill such an important role, but great currents and tides and crashing waves are not necessary to feel the magic of water. Director Larry Dolphin says that of all the areas of the nature center, the pond is the most visited and the most used. A small dock invites visitors to approach, and a few canoes and kayaks are kept nearby. Just a few dips of the paddle and one is floating in a mirrored realm between sky and earth, surrounded by natural things. It doesn't take long for even the novice to begin to feel at home. Streams and rivers and lakes may call to those with acquired skills, but a pond is a fine and gentle place to start.

With the guidance of the nature center staff, the pond is also a place for observing, collecting, and identifying. Crayfish and giant water-bugs, freshwater shrimp, water boatmen, water scorpions—countless small and living things that inhabit an unknown world as complex as our own are waiting to be found. Remarkably, since its creation, all the pond's residents have found their way there on their own—none planted or transported. In the spring, a pair or two of Canada geese nest beside the pond, and the chance to watch the goslings swim and grow and discover their world is another treat. Spring migration also brings the perfectly painted wood ducks and green and blue winged teal, who know the pond as a valuable stopover on their way to their own nesting grounds.

Much of the beauty of the natural world is about edges and borders. The pond itself is framed by water-loving willows and cottonwoods. Just a few feet away lies the prairie that enfolds and surrounds the pond, made more complex and complete by this interface. Here the goldenrod and blazing star, blue spiderwort, white indigo and black-eyed Susans hold forth. Here, too, is the Cope's gray tree frog—

CHAPTER 4

A snapping turtle moves slowly through the grass on its way to the water.

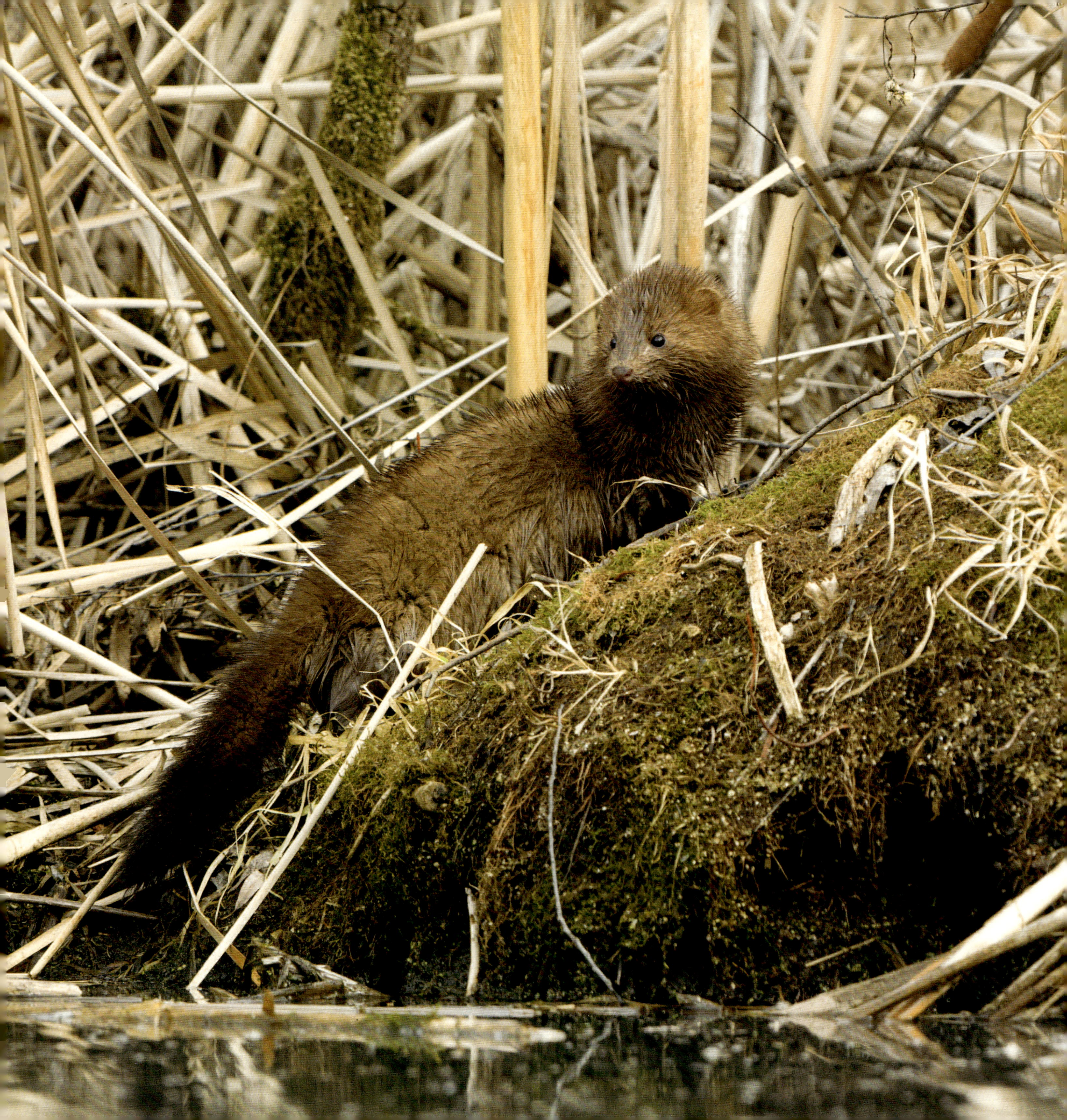

CHAPTER 4

a fine singer on spring and summer evenings who doesn't live *in* the pond as his cousins do, but who still prefers water nearby. The same can be said of monarch butterflies and bobolinks, pheasants and brown-headed cowbirds, song sparrows and dickcissels. All are prairie residents who enjoy the proximity of a pond.

Just beyond the prairie lies the dark wall of the woods, and within it the banks of Dobbins Creek—more edges, more borders, more interplay of ecosystems and species. It is within this interwoven tapestry of life that the landscape of the Hormel Nature Center displays its richness, and fulfills its role in providing vital habitat and a diversity of green space. The center itself is an "edge" of sorts, an interface between a modern, bustling community and a much older, quieter natural community. The interstate highway, only a short distance away, provides another edge; and when the breeze is out of the south, the hum and rumble can be easily heard, a reminder of the speed and hurly-burly of modern life, and all that goes with it.

But sometimes on a quiet evening beside still waters, as the sunset paints its palette, as the moon and stars cast their reflections, there is a more ancient, more primeval music. Cottonwood leaves quiver. There is the buzz of a dragonfly, the rattle of a kingfisher, the rising song of the chorus frogs. It is the rich and varied song of life, of all watery places. A little man-made pond on the prairie is a part of it. And it is good to have a place to listen.

A mallard rests among dandelions on a hiking trail adjacent to the pond.

Opposite: A mink scans its surroundings after emerging from the water.

CHAPTER 4

Thick vegetation surrounds the pond in midsummer, giving wildlife an abundance of protective cover.

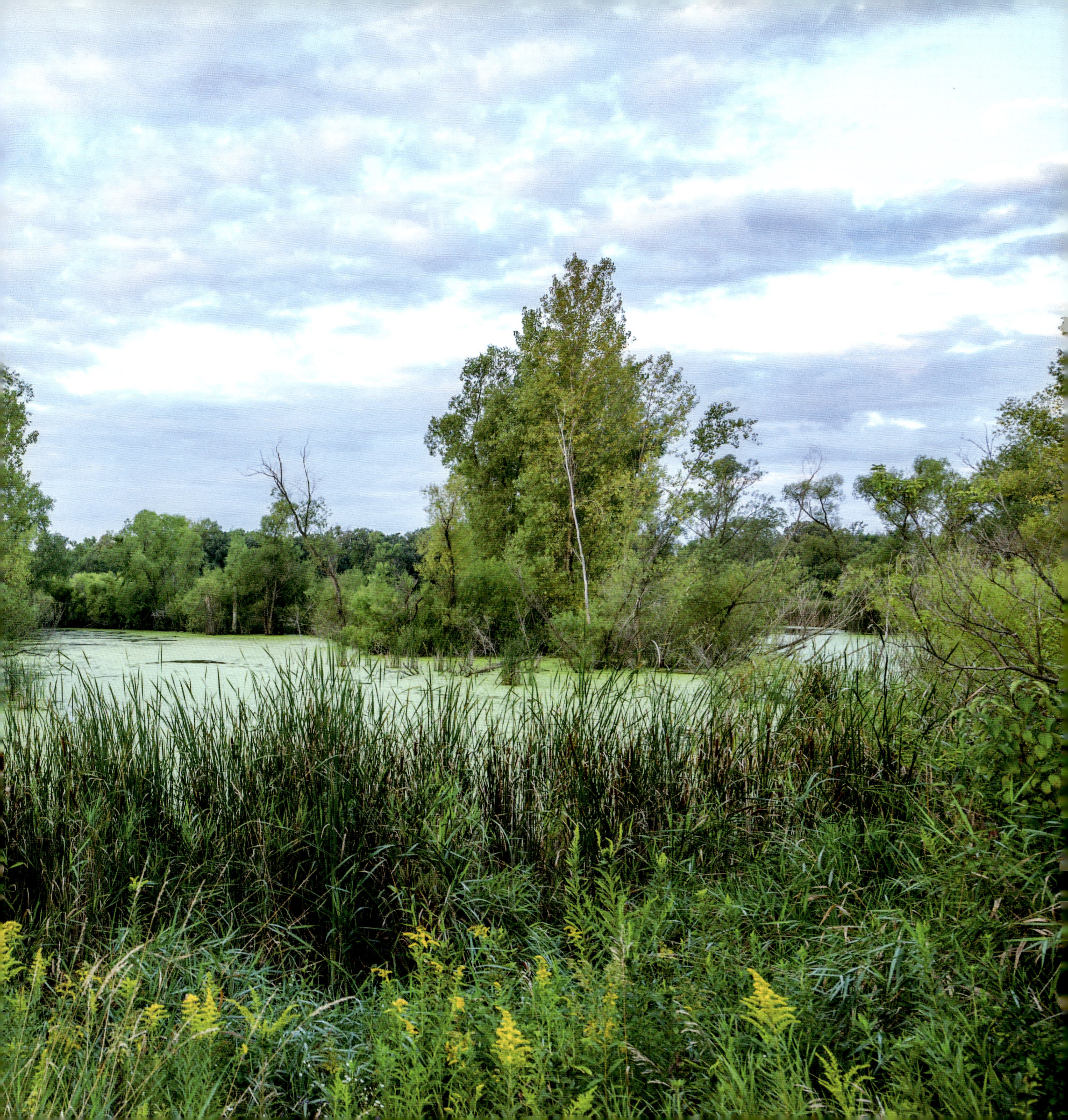

CHAPTER 4

A green frog emerges from the water to take in the warmth of the sun.

CHAPTER 4

A Cope's gray tree frog clings to a branch near the pond's edge.

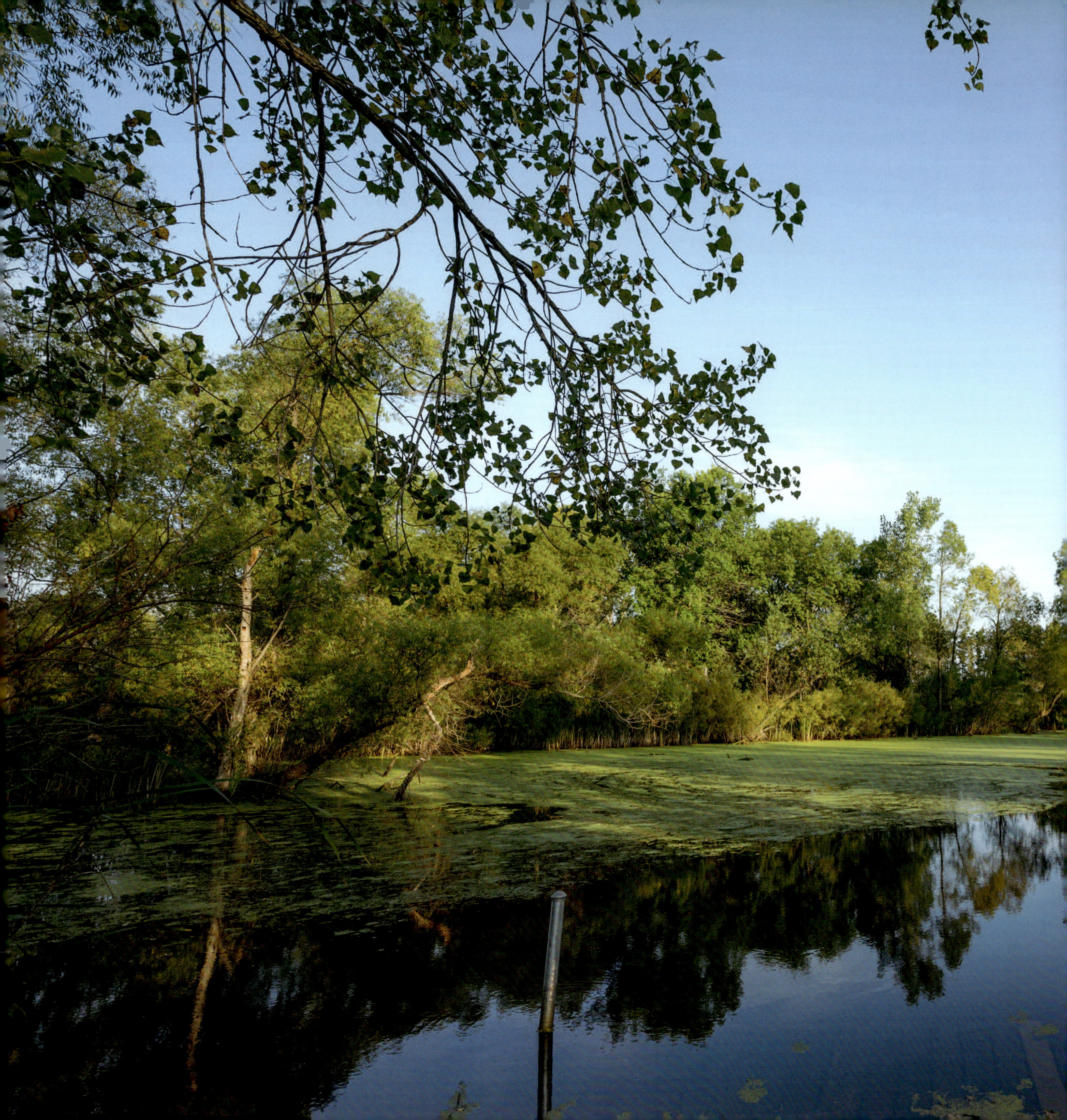

CHAPTER 4

Two poles mark the location of the dock in the flooded pond.

CHAPTER 4

A mallard hen vigorously flaps her wings, drying her feathers.

CHAPTER 4

A green-winged teal swims in the vibrant blue water of the pond in early spring.

CHAPTER 4

The sun rises over a hiking trail near the northeast corner of the pond.

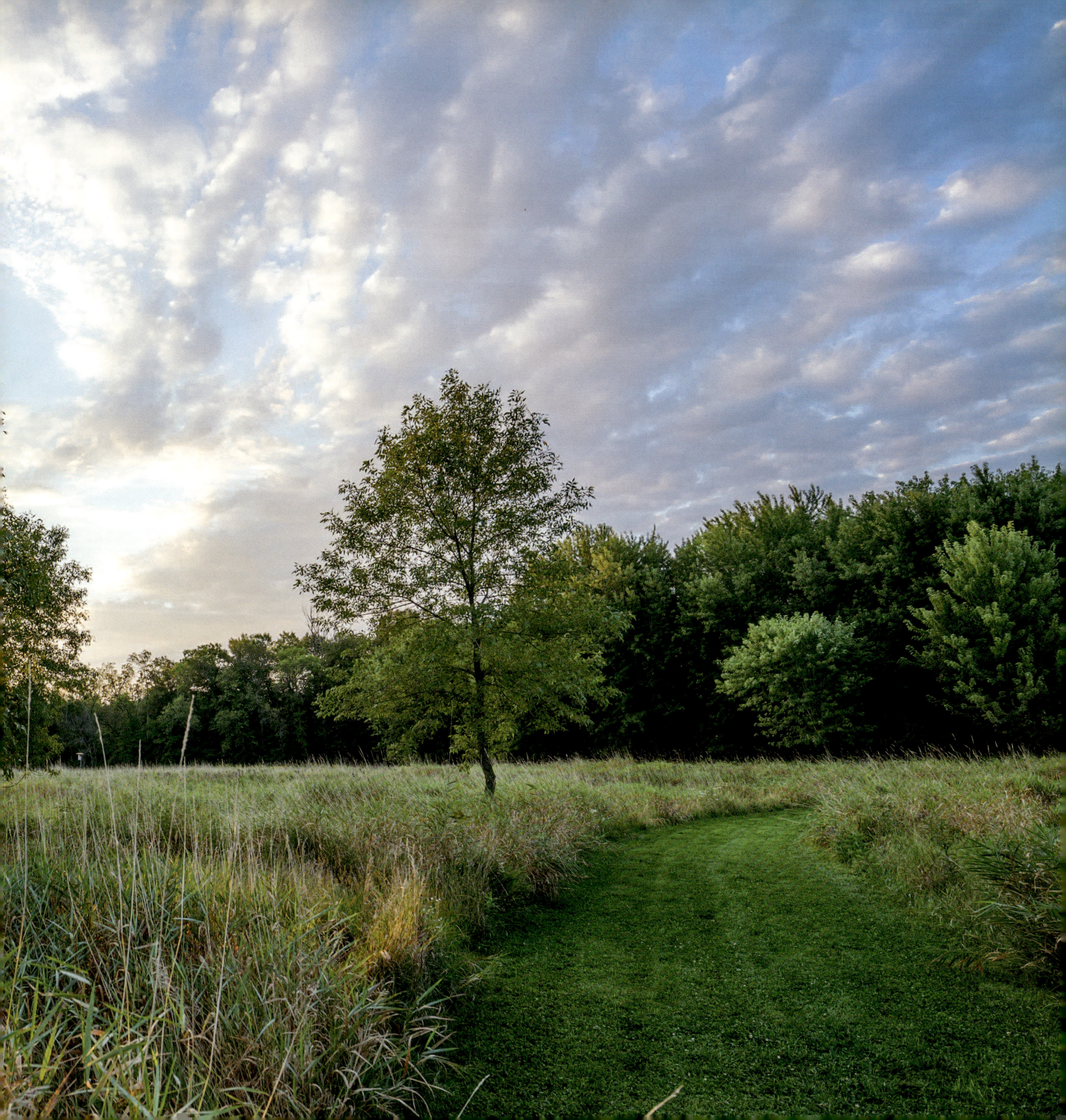

CHAPTER 4

CHAPTER 4

Top: A blue dasher looks over the prairie from a sturdy perch.

Bottom: A twelve-spotted skimmer sits on a cattail just above the water's surface.

Opposite: A Hagen's bluet damselfly cleans itself while clinging to a prairie plant.

CHAPTER 4

A pair of goslings compete for an earthworm.

CHAPTER 4

Goslings playfully fight with one another in mid-May.

CHAPTER 4

Blue-winged teal arrive at the pond in early spring, staying for only a short time before nesting elsewhere.

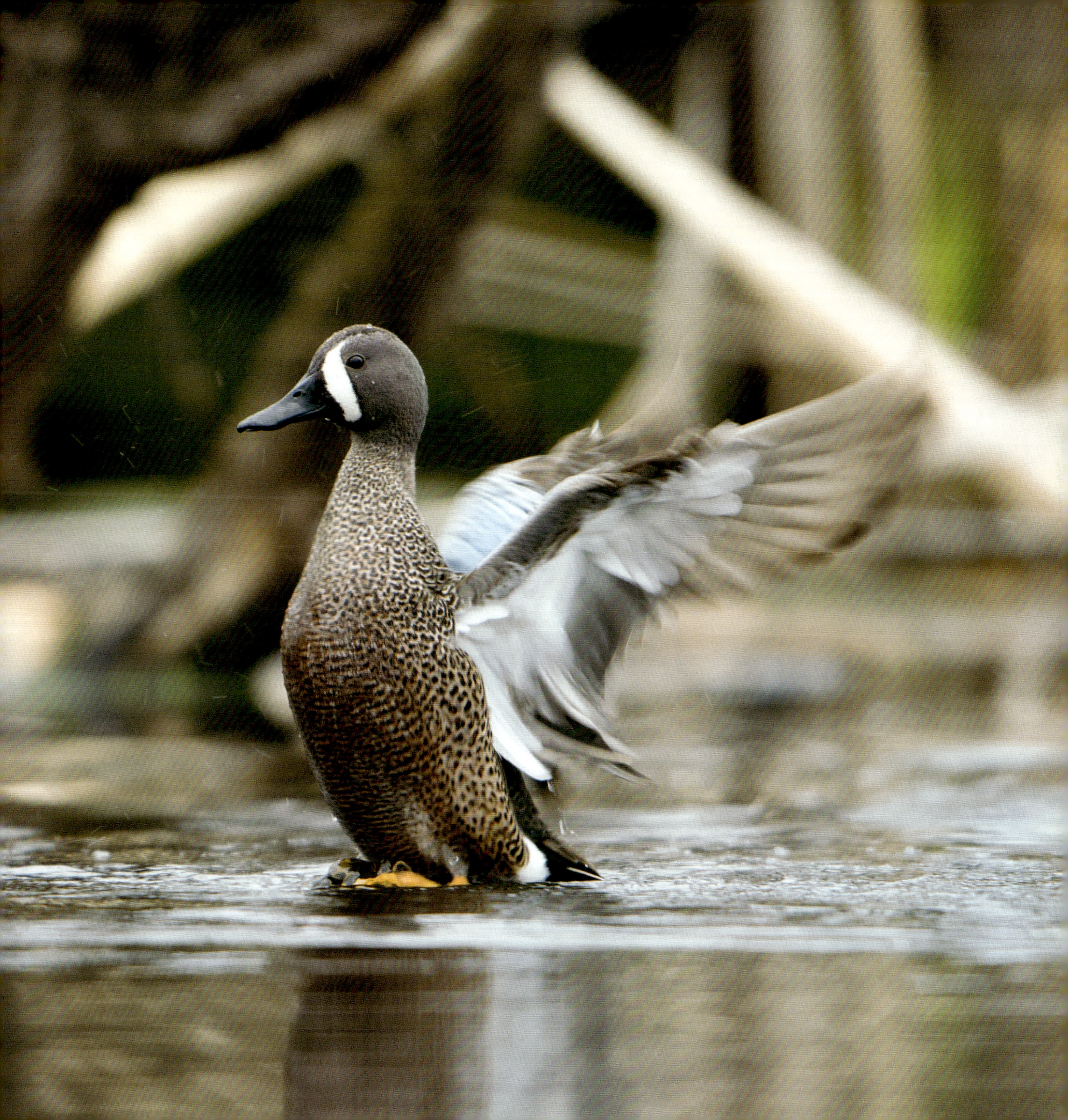

CHAPTER 4

Usually seen low to the ground and in dense vegetation, a sora moves along the thick growth near the edge of the pond.

CHAPTER 4

A common yellowthroat, more often heard than seen, hides among the stalks of cattails.

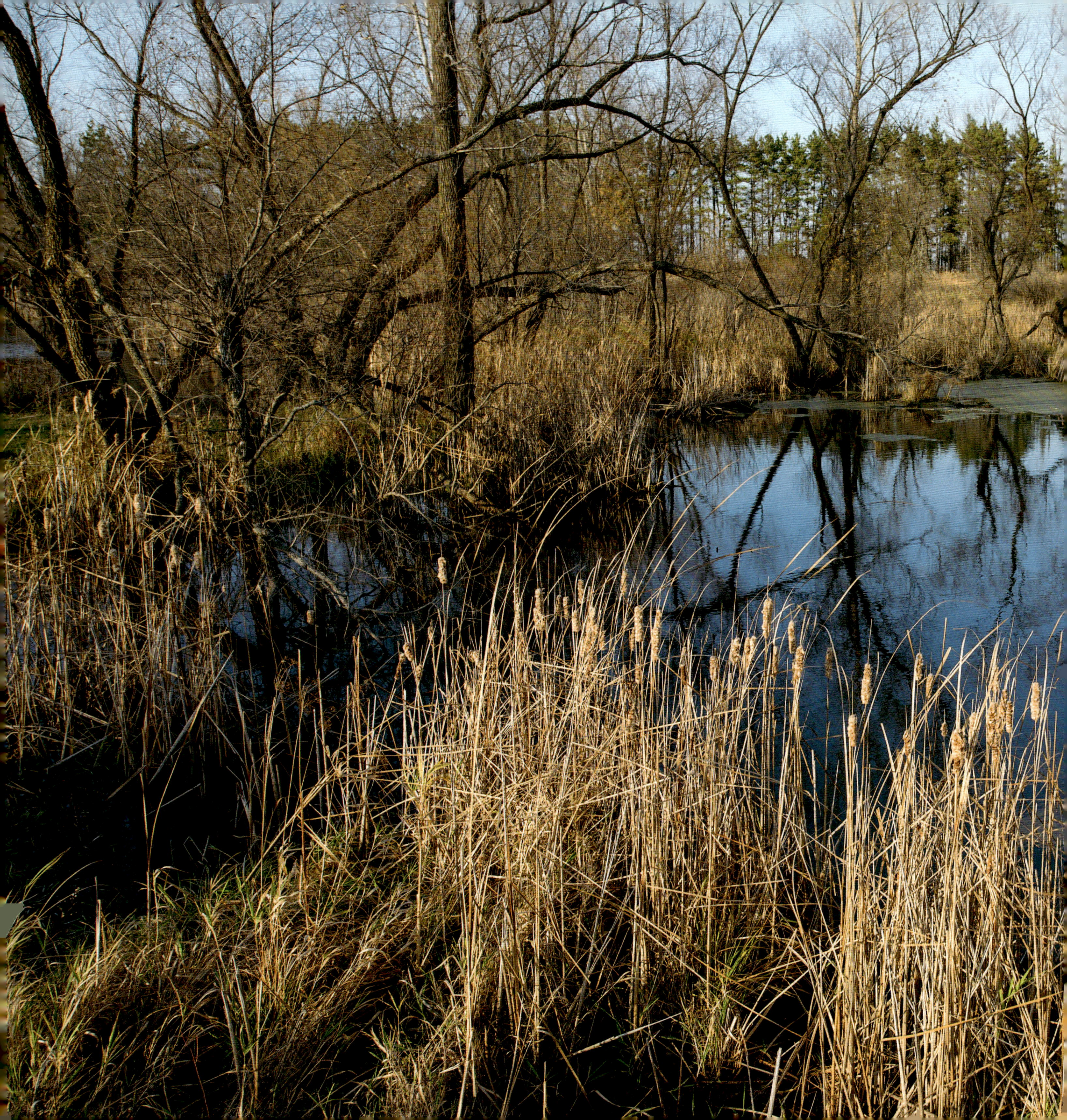

CHAPTER 4

The reflective surface of the pond mirrors the sky as the early November sun warms the earth.

CHAPTER 4

CHAPTER 4

A green heron walks up the trunk of a fallen tree, searching for small fish, frogs, and aquatic insects in the water below.

Opposite: A dead snapping turtle lies on the roots of an overturned tree.

CHAPTER 4

In late March, the ice has melted off the surface of the pond, and only patches of recent snow remain.

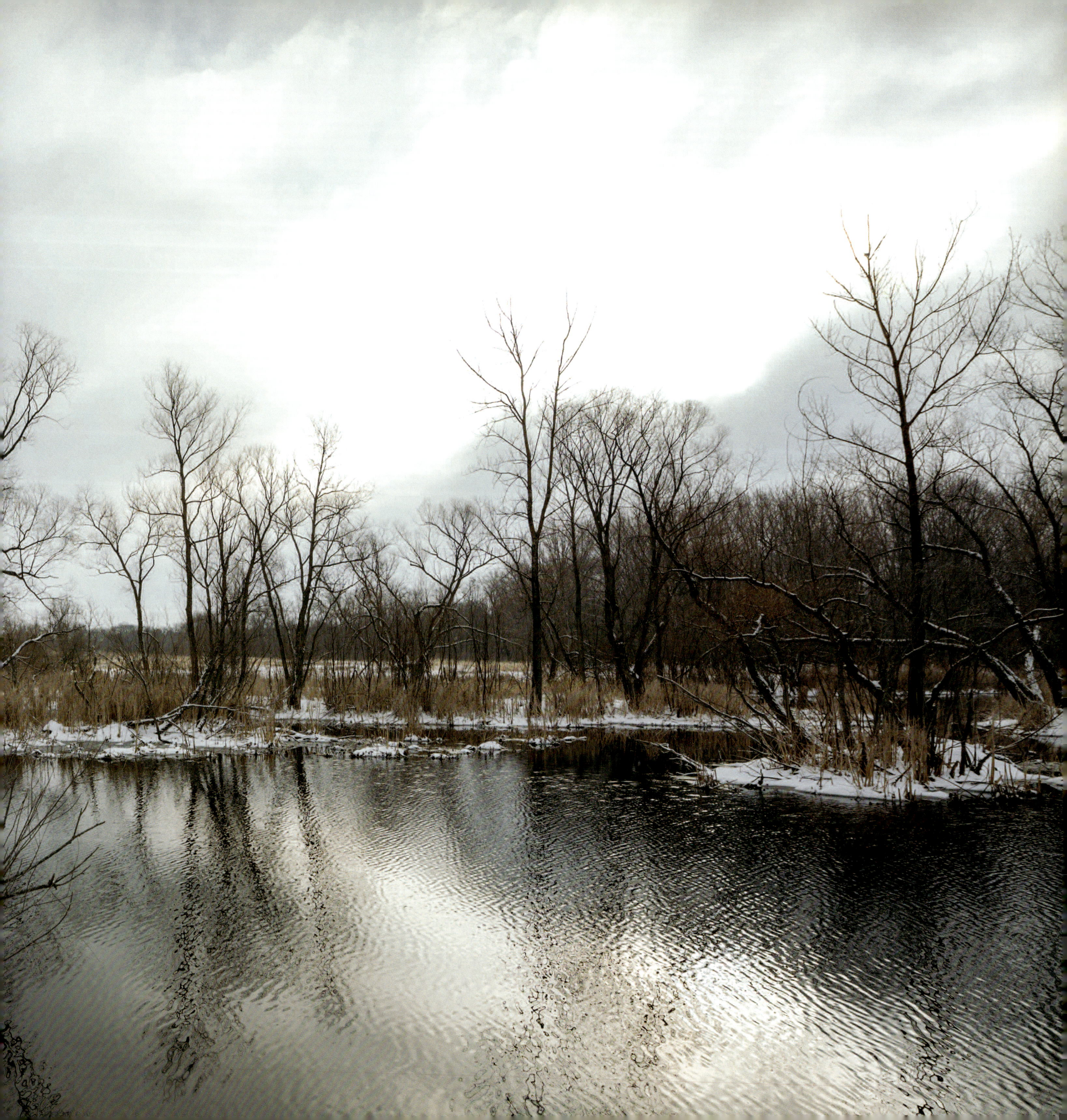

CHAPTER 4

CHAPTER 4

Top: A pair of Canada geese rest in the sun while keeping a watchful eye out for predators.

Bottom: A female goose sits on her clutch of eggs during an April snowstorm.

Opposite: Safe from the wind and rain, a young gosling peers out from under its mother's wings.

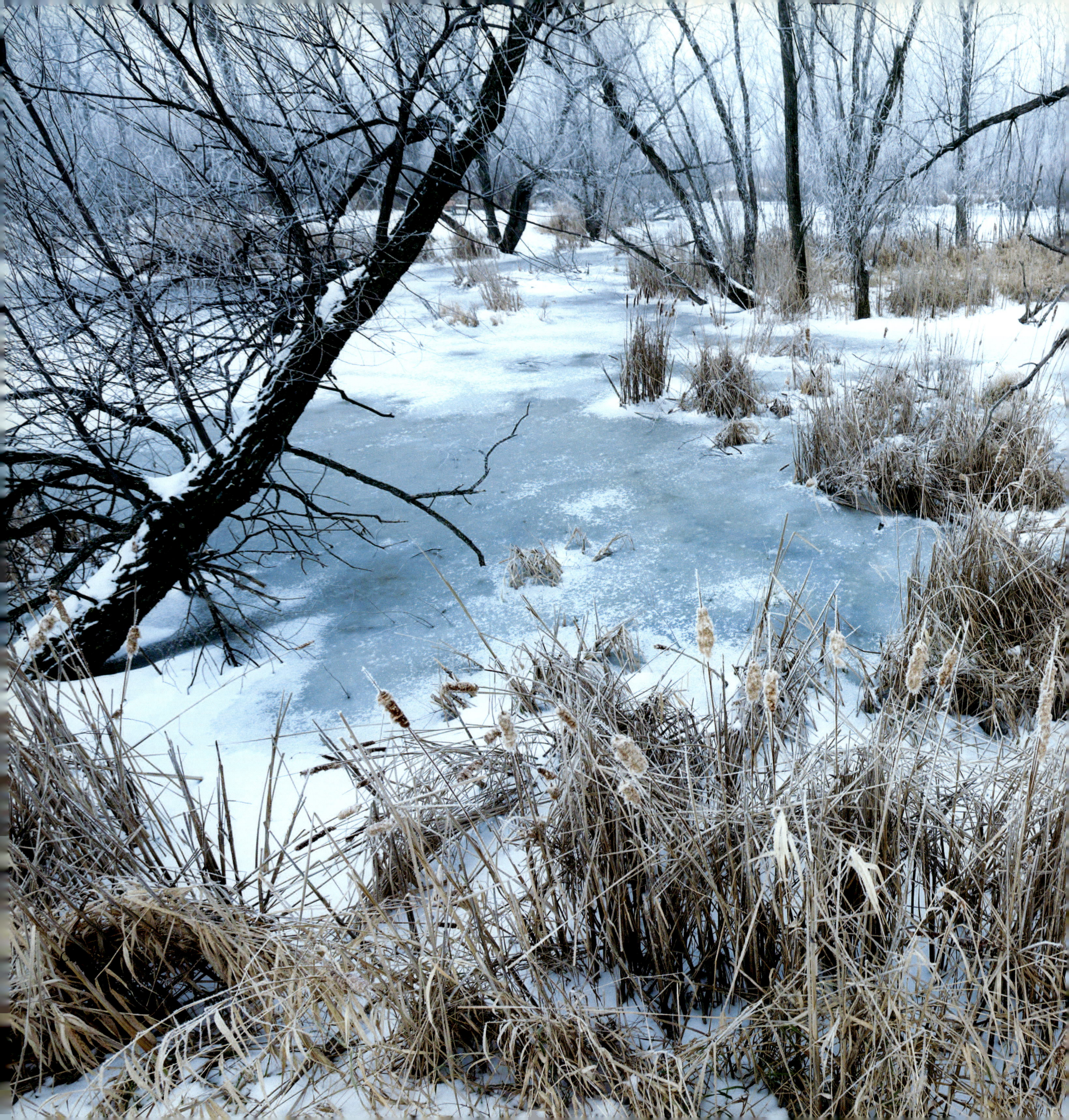

CHAPTER 4

A frozen pond sits covered in frost as winter takes hold of the land.

A bench catches the first rays of light as the sun warms the West Prairie.

It's not what you look at that matters, it's what you see.

—Henry David Thoreau

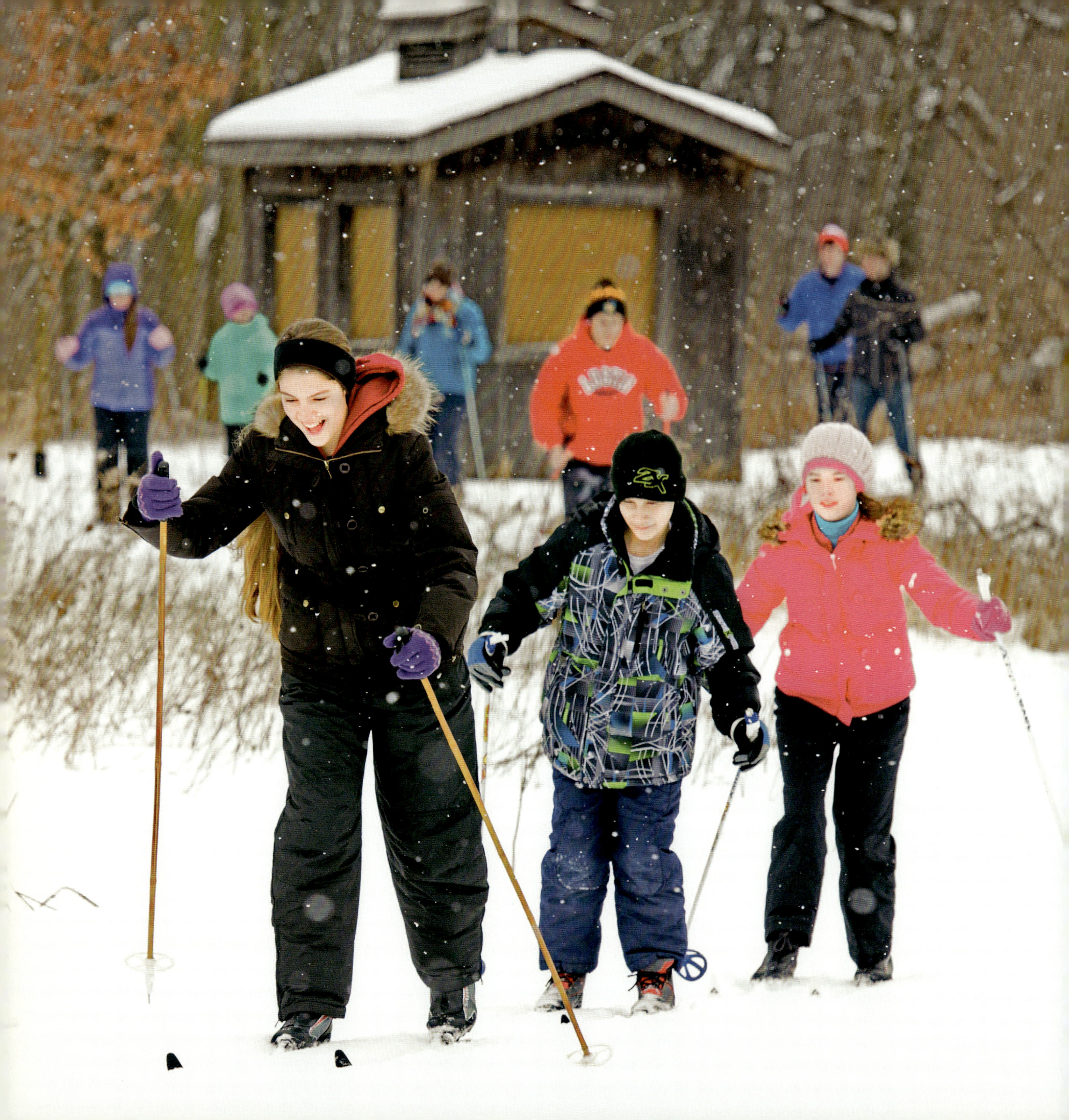

CHAPTER 5

Connecting People With The Land: Education, Conservation, Magic

One visits a nature center to get close to nature. That's the whole idea, really. And it usually works. In some small way, through some combination of sunshine, rain, snow, wind, walking, running, paddling, sitting, looking, listening, and smelling, something usually happens during an outing. It probably wouldn't have happened somewhere else—at least not in the house or in the car—something that connects one a little more closely to the natural world.

To be sure, there are many other places where this might happen—a park, a city street, a garden, in the countryside. Even in your own backyard. But to go to a place expressly designed and intended to bring you closer to nature and to help you learn something about it—well, that's a different thing. There is an intent involved, on the part of the builders and the keepers and the teachers of the center, and on the part of the visitor—who must say, in some quiet voice in the back of his or her mind, "I want to go and feel something. I want to learn something." And then to decide that the nature center is the place to do it.

This conscious intent shapes everything, from how the trails and pond and woods are shaped and kept and maintained, to how buildings and displays are created and arranged, to how the staff interacts with the public, to the attitude with which visitors arrive. A common goal and theme runs through it all, though it may often be unspoken. And with this common goal and intent—to get people closer to nature—it is not unusual for something special to happen, in the heart or in the mind.

But some other element must be there as well, something besides all the careful planning and arranging and intending. Something . . . dare we say, magic? And that part—the magic—is where nature herself steps in. For the center is but a window, a doorway—carefully kept and maintained, to be sure—through which one may glimpse, or even enter, the natural world and all the magic contained therein.

Different people are attracted to different doorways. For some it may be the stream—Dobbins Creek—and the chance to stand on a footbridge or sit on a rock and listen to the music of flowing water. It is impossible to say how sitting and quietly watching a heron, who stands and quietly watches you, changes a person. But it can. So can the sunlit glitter of a riffle, the flash of a kingfisher, the stealthy movement of a mink. It is not a common thing, anymore, to rest beside a stream and to let its music echo within you. After eons of evolution, our minds and bodies and spirits are still attuned to the song of the stream and the visions that accompany it. But it is not so easy to find the song and the visions anymore. A nature center can lead you back to the magic of flowing water.

Cross-country skiing is a popular winter activity. School groups come from all over Mower County to glide across the nature center's groomed trails.

CHAPTER 5

For others the doorway may be a small blanket of restored prairie, where big bluestem grass and goldenrod and leadplant and blazing star and coreopsis and black-eyed Susan bloom beneath the sky, just as they did for the long, uncounted millennia before the arrival of the plow. Where a marsh hawk or a red-tailed hawk dips and soars, or a red fox glides, and where the mind's eye can almost spy the looming figure of a bison within the tall grass. That can be magic.

For some the pond is the inviting doorway—the chance to sit on a dock or to float in a small craft, absorbing all the images and sounds and smells of a wet and wild place, all the richness of life it supports. A dragonfly landing on the bow of a canoe—or on your knee or on your head—can change the way you look at the whole world. With their multifaceted, jeweled eyes, dragonflies do not see the way that we do. And those who take the time to look long at dragonflies do not see the same way either. Perhaps they have been touched by magic.

And there are many for whom the forest is the door of choice. The woods were the original doorway for Jay Hormel, the link back to his childhood and his gift to future children. In planting his trees, in imagining the shaded trails to come, he touched the future and generations yet unborn. Now those generations walk those trails, listen to the song of the cardinal, see the sunlight streaming through the green canopy. Is that not magic—generations of the past, present, and future, linked by one person's vision and by the growth of living things?

And so it is that magic is always present at the Hormel Nature Center, never far away. But sometimes it is helpful to be introduced—to be gently ushered into the theater, to be told the names of the actors and the players, what to watch and listen for, and what it all means. It can help to have a teacher or a guide, especially for young visitors.

The Jay C. Hormel Nature Center has a long history of introducing young people to the wonders of nature, with structured programs designed to meet identifiable goals and objectives. Grade-level programming begins with the visits of kindergartners who explore the use of all their senses in the outdoor environment. First graders are introduced to the basic concepts of "living and non-living." Second graders learn how seeds reproduce and travel, and also participate in apple cidering. In the third grade, students learn about the complexities and realities of predator-prey relationships and deer habitat, and they are introduced to orienteering and mapping.

By the time students reach the fourth grade, many are ready for a more intense hands-on experience, for the opportunity to participate in some old-fashioned "work" of the sort that has long connected people to the natural world and the cycle of the seasons. Maple syruping fills the bill perfectly. In addition to tapping and collecting and the sweet-smelling process of boiling down sap in the sugar shack, kids also learn how trees "work." Understanding such things is another powerful way to truly *feel* the connection between human beings and nature, while reinforcing a connection to the past.

Fifth-grade students explore the science of adaptation in the natural world. They try the time-honored winter activities of cross-country skiing and snowshoeing, and help with bird observation,

CHAPTER 5

A student in a bird banding class watches a downy woodpecker that has been captured in a banding trap.

identification, and banding at the feeders. They also participate in fire building and winter survival exercises.

In the seventh grade, students gain a deeper understanding of nature by taking part in the study of Dobbins Creek, through water quality testing and the monitoring of macro-invertebrates and "indicator species" like the caddis fly, Mayfly, and crane fly nymphs—the presence or absence of which helps to indicate the health of a stream.

Perhaps it goes without saying that through all these student education programs, there is a good chance that here and there our old friend, magic, may creep in unexpectedly.

The opportunities for education and participation at the center reach far beyond school programs for students. The primary goal is to get people outdoors and connect them to their environment. There are community education adventures, field trips, and canoe outings. Service organizations, Scouts, 4-H, and others help with land management, trail maintenance, and chores, including removal of invasive species like buckthorn, promotion of oak regeneration, and propagation of maples near the sugar shack. And there is the long-established and continuing series of public programs and nature-related concerts in the Ruby Rupner Auditorium.

All of these activities and programs share common goals, and make up what director Larry Dolphin refers to as the three-legged stool. First, the Environmental Education component increases awareness and knowledge of the natural world and all its systems, leading to clarity and understanding of environmental issues, and the ability to make well-informed decisions. The second leg is Conservation Education—the understanding of our limited resources and how they interact, and the instilling of a set of values to guide the wise use of those resources. The third leg, Outdoor Education in all its many facets, simply involves getting people outdoors, in as many ways and for as many reasons as possible. For once someone is outdoors, nature herself is always the ultimate teacher, and a respect and affection for nature is the eventual outcome.

All of these facets are represented in the center's mission statement: "To embrace and encourage environmental education, scientific opportunities, and the enjoyment of nature at the Jay C. Hormel Nature Center." And of course, if a little magic is discovered, that's probably okay, too.

It has been a long and winding journey for this small and lovely bit of stream-side landscape, from prairie to farmland to country estate to arboretum to nature center. It is a story no one could have predicted. But the story of this human interaction with the land has not ended. It will continue in many ways and in directions yet unknown. One of the next steps can be clearly seen. Soon after the publication of this book that looks back on the nature center's history, a grand multi-million dollar interpretive center will take its place on the land, looking across the prairie and over the woods toward Dobbins Creek. The new building will be three times the size of the old one, designed to

CHAPTER 5

A student assists director Larry Dolphin in filtering the freshly made apple cider.

CHAPTER 5

Dobbins Creek gently flows under a walking bridge toward the Cedar River.

CHAPTER 5

reflect and enhance the purposes and mission of the Jay C. Hormel Nature Center. It will be a new doorway, helping to connect the people of the Austin, Minnesota area to their land, their history, and to all the unnamed wonders of the natural world.

When one imagines the new center, or walks beside the creek under the arched, green ceiling of a mature woods, or sits beside the pond looking out over a field of wildflowers, or listens in as a class of first graders gasp at some small miracle of nature, it is easy to imagine that Jay Hormel and his trusty tree planter, Roy Anderson, would smilingly approve.

Sculpted by Minnesota artist Christopher Tully, the "Welcome Circle" sits just steps from the parking lot and provides a map of the property.

CHAPTER 5

Chimney swifts, birds that nest in chimneys and hollow trees, use this nesting tower as a site for raising their young.

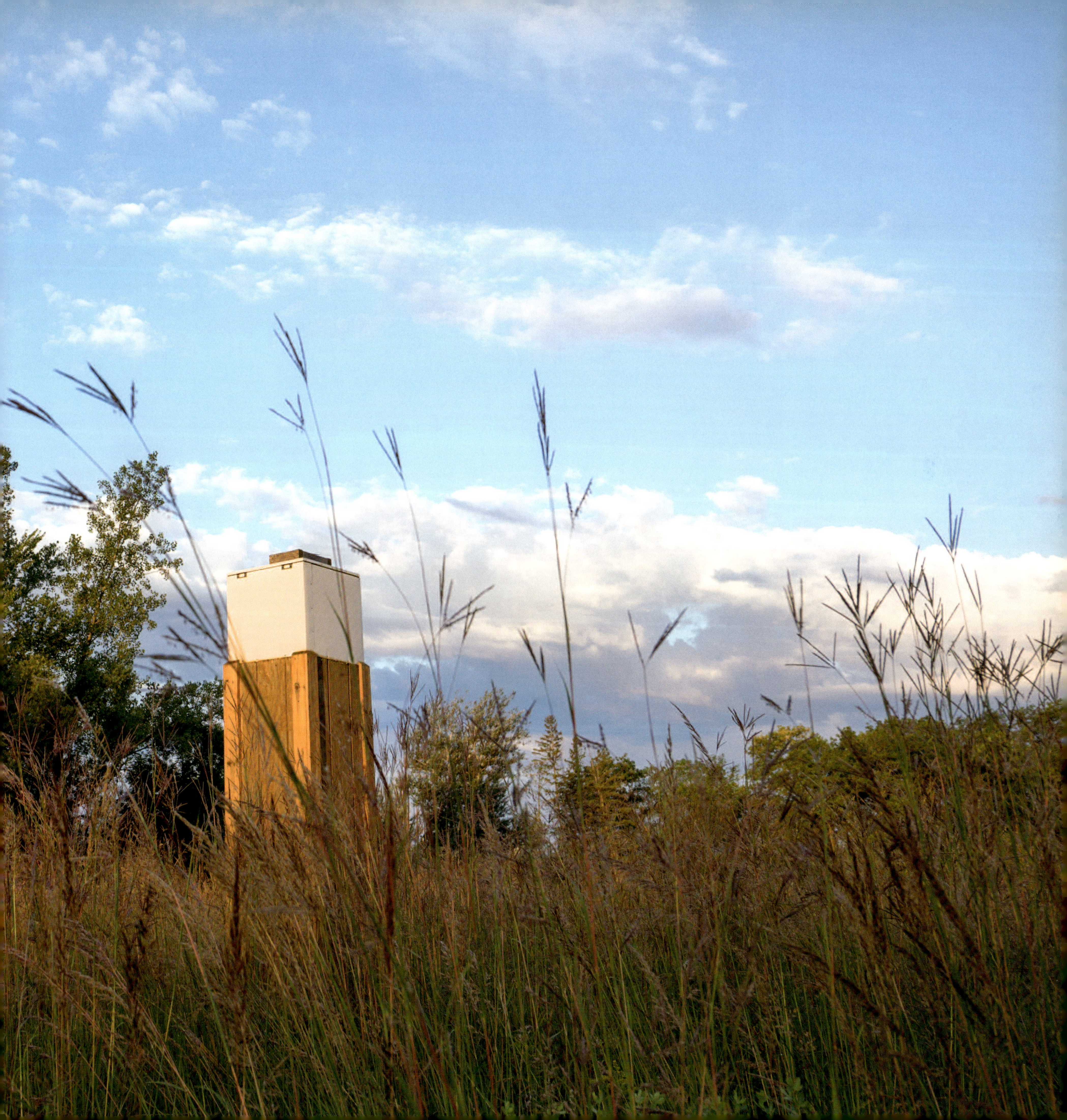

CHAPTER 5

Nature center volunteers strategically place eastern bluebird houses throughout the prairies.

Opposite: An American robin nests on a wooden beam protruding from the log cabin.

CHAPTER 5

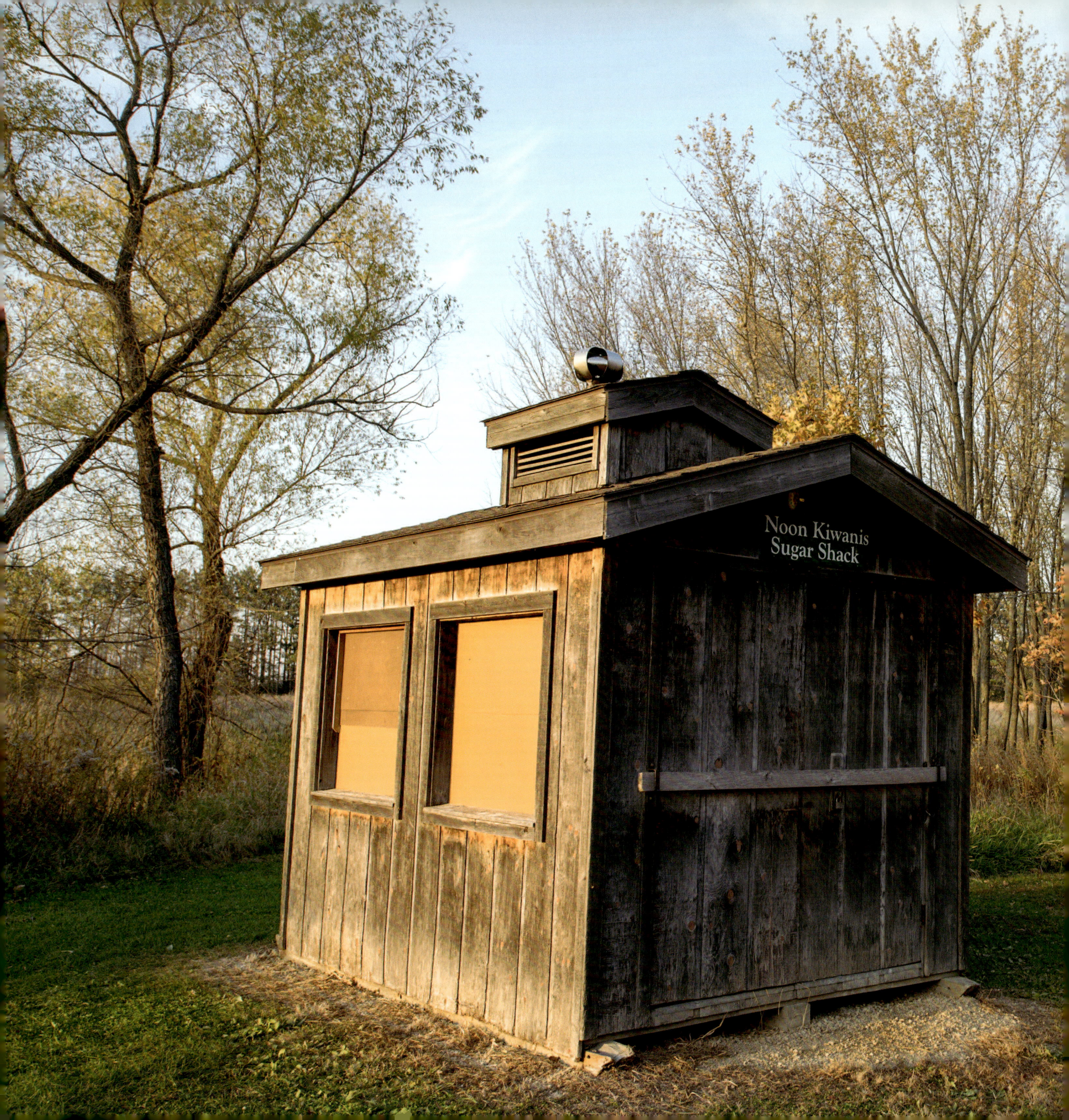
Noon Kiwanis
Sugar Shack

CHAPTER 5

The Noon Kiwanis Sugar Shack sits beside a grove of maple trees that will produce enough sap to boil down into maple syrup.

CHAPTER 5

In March, buckets are placed on tapped maple trees to collect sap.

CHAPTER 5

In a matter of hours, spring weather in southeastern Minnesota can drastically alter the landscape.

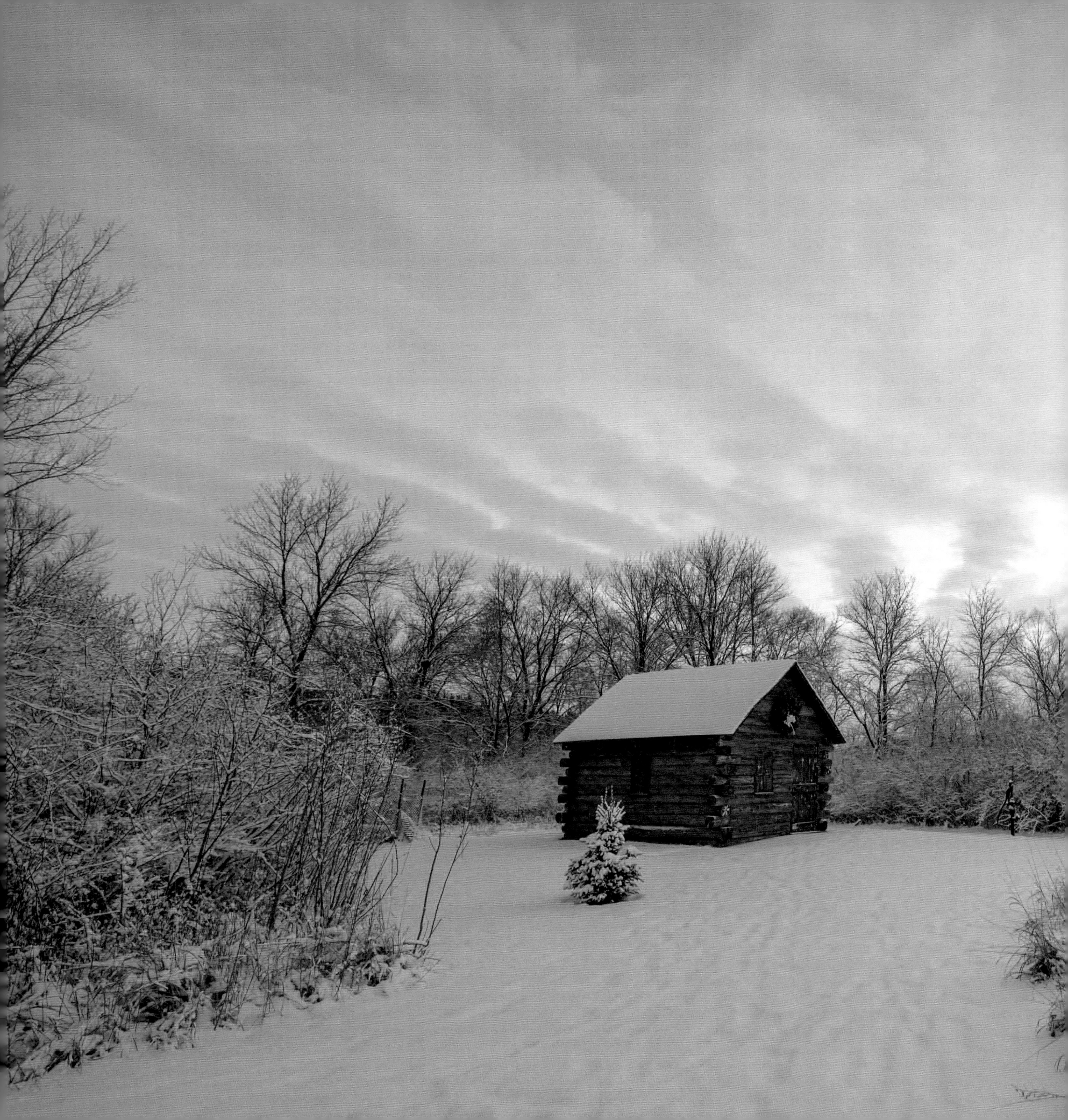

CHAPTER 5

The log cabin carries a fresh blanket of snow after a winter snowstorm.

CHAPTER 5

Covered in a thick layer of frost, the observation tower and surrounding landscape sit cloaked in white.

CHAPTER 5

Fresh snow covers the hiking trail leading to the covered bridge.

CHAPTER 5

Children watch a spotted fawn emerge from the thick prairie grass.

CHAPTER 5

Two fawns, orphaned at an early age, feed on the grasses and plants in a field just north of the parking lot.

CHAPTER 5

The Jacques Chipault Memorial Trail, dedicated as a handicapped access trail in 1992, leads away from the visitor center and into the forest.

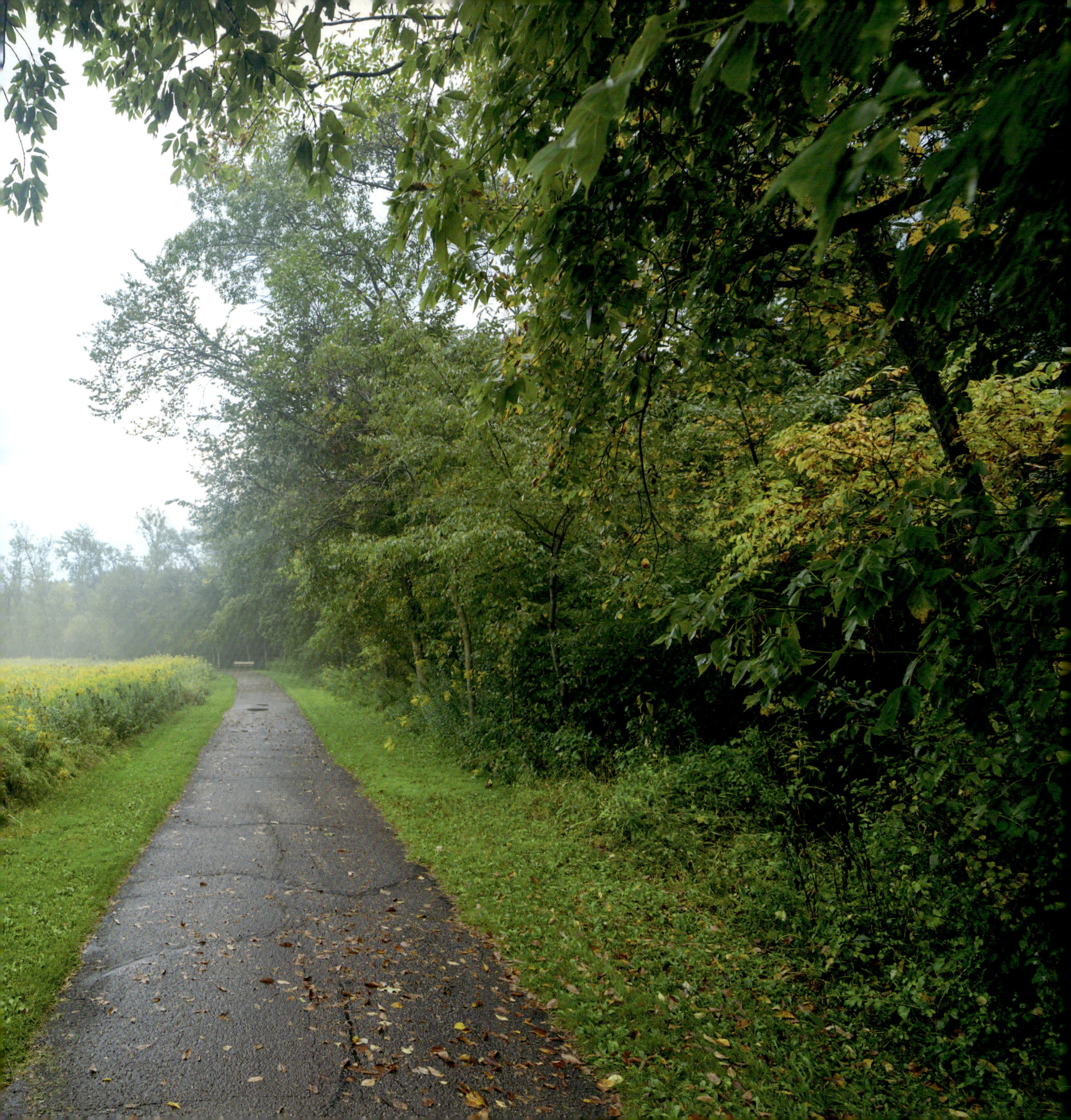

CHAPTER 5

CHAPTER 5

Banding songbirds for research purposes, Larry Dolphin reaches into a bird banding cage and inspects a black-capped chickadee.

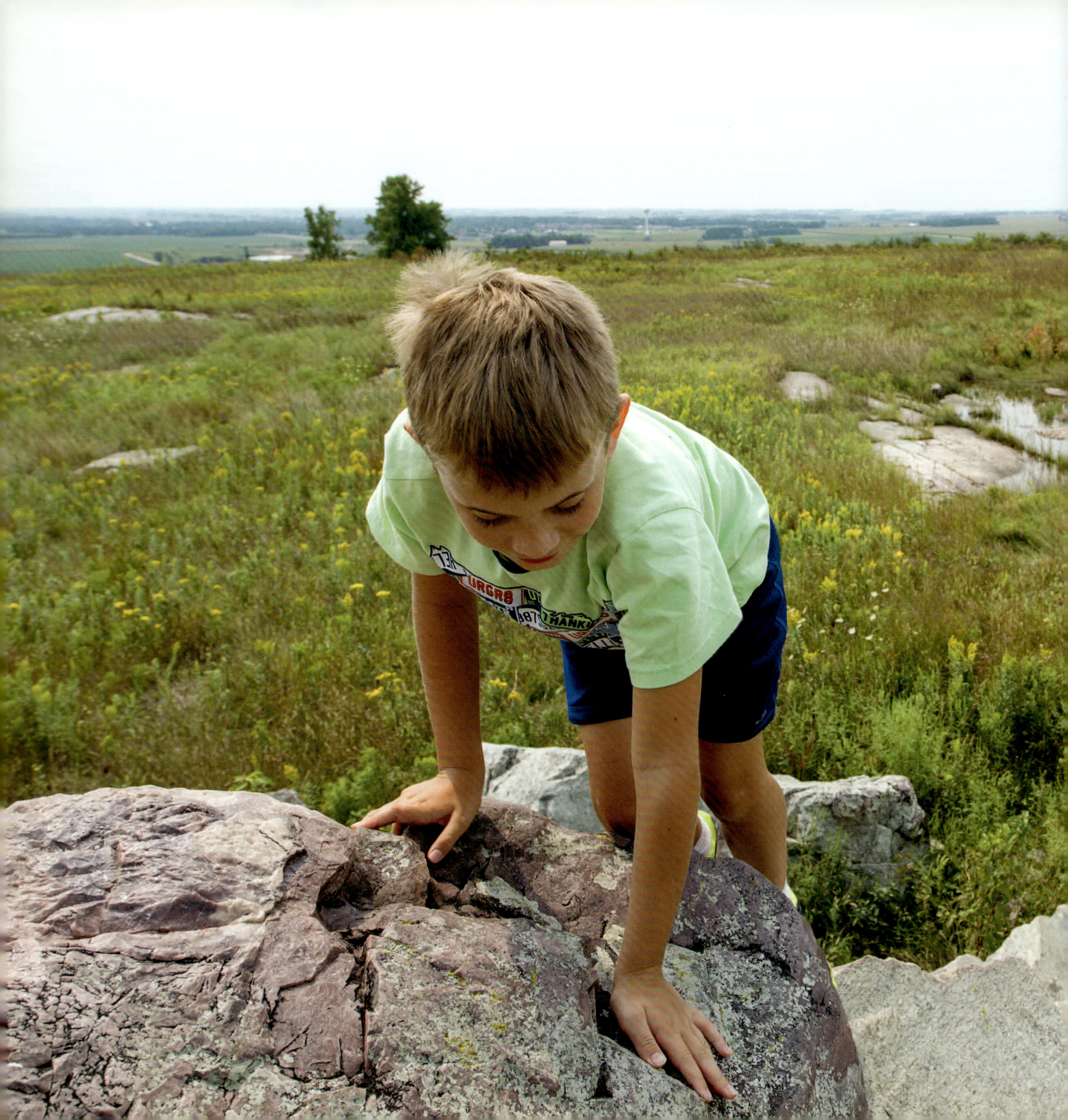

CHAPTER 5

During the summer, participants in the nature center's outdoor education classes are offered the opportunity to see different parts of southern Minnesota, including the Root River, Eagle Bluff Environmental Learning Center, and in this image, Blue Mounds State Park.

CHAPTER 5

Naturalist Maria Anderson carries a butterfly net, looking to capture, tag, and release monarch butterflies.

CHAPTER 5

A student in a monarch tagging class pulls a vibrant monarch from a butterfly net.

CHAPTER 5

During a canoe and kayak trip on the Root River, students dock their watercraft and search for aquatic insects in riffle areas.

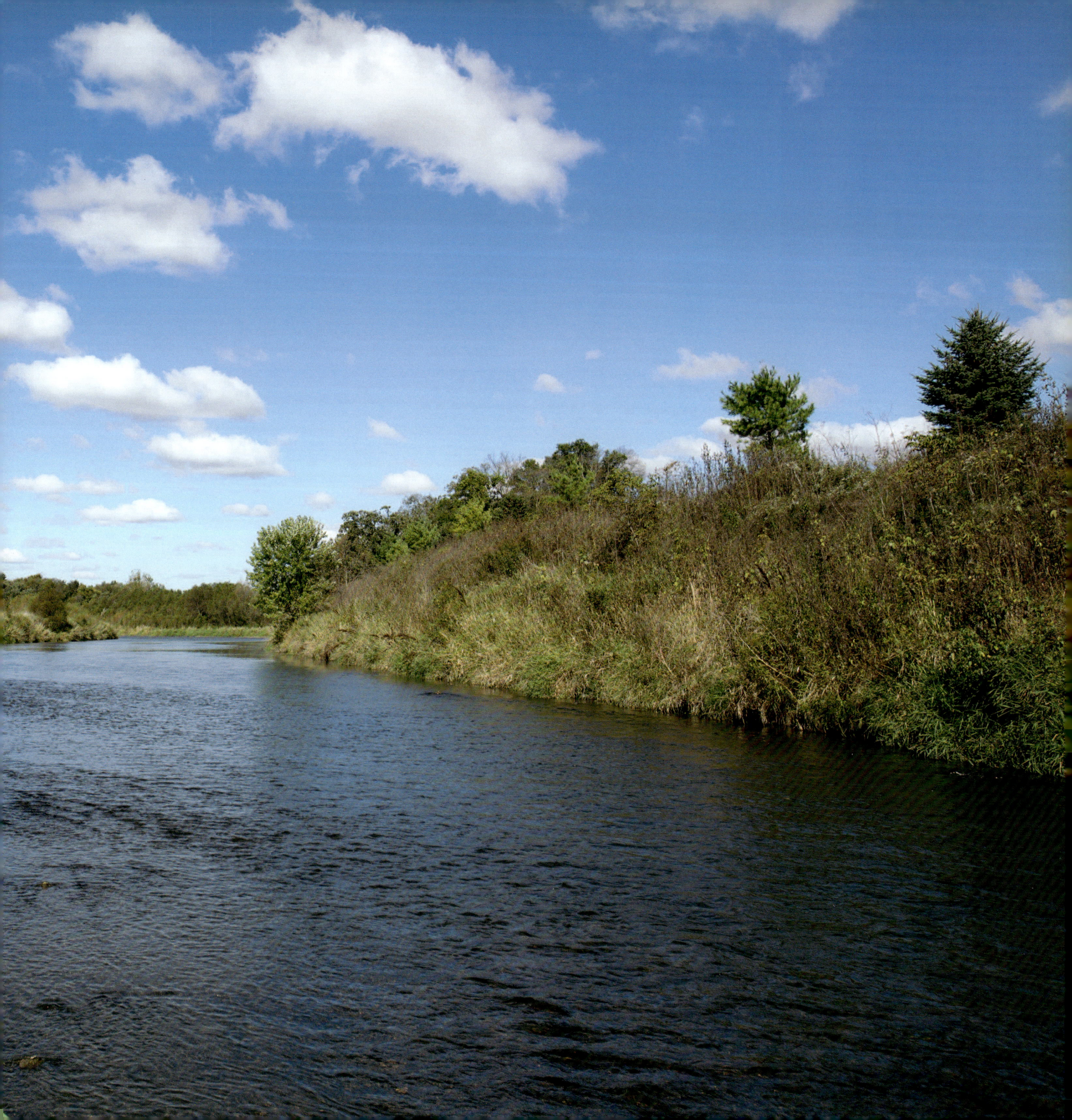

CHAPTER 5

Former intern Tom Butusov collects seeds from prairie plants to be used for future plantings.

CHAPTER 5

Office Manager Julie Champlin places Guka, the barred owl, on his outdoor perch. Guka is the nature center's educational bird of prey.

CHAPTER 5

Director Larry Dolphin demonstrates where to look for aquatic insects in Dobbins Creek as students hold nets to catch the insects as they move downstream.

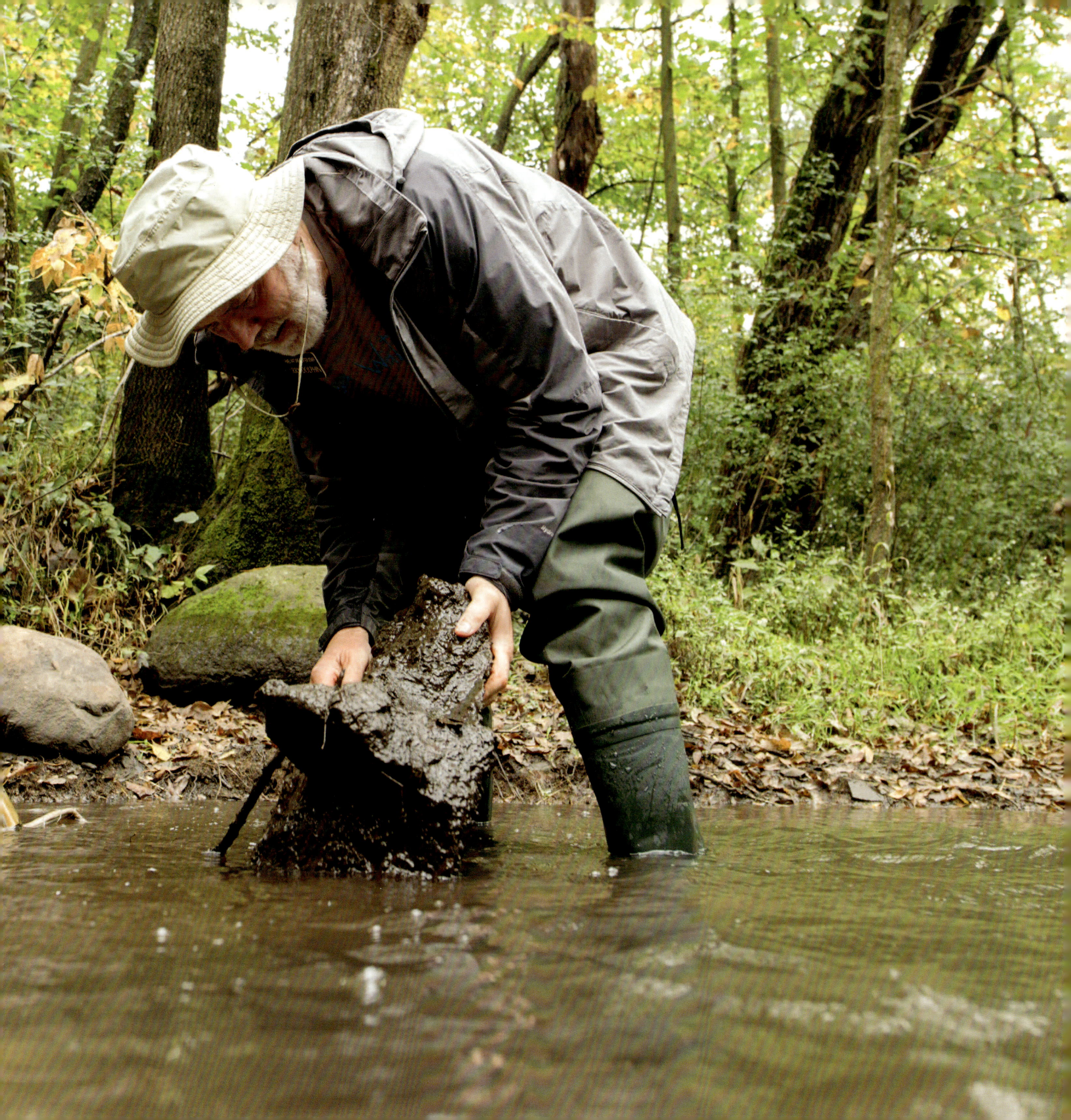

CHAPTER 5

A student examines his recent catch of crayfish from Dobbins Creek.

CHAPTER 5

Immersed in a field of goldenrod, a student in a monarch tagging class swings his net as monarchs scatter.

CHAPTER 5

Land Manager Mike Goetz leads a prairie burn, an essential element of the landscape's overall health.

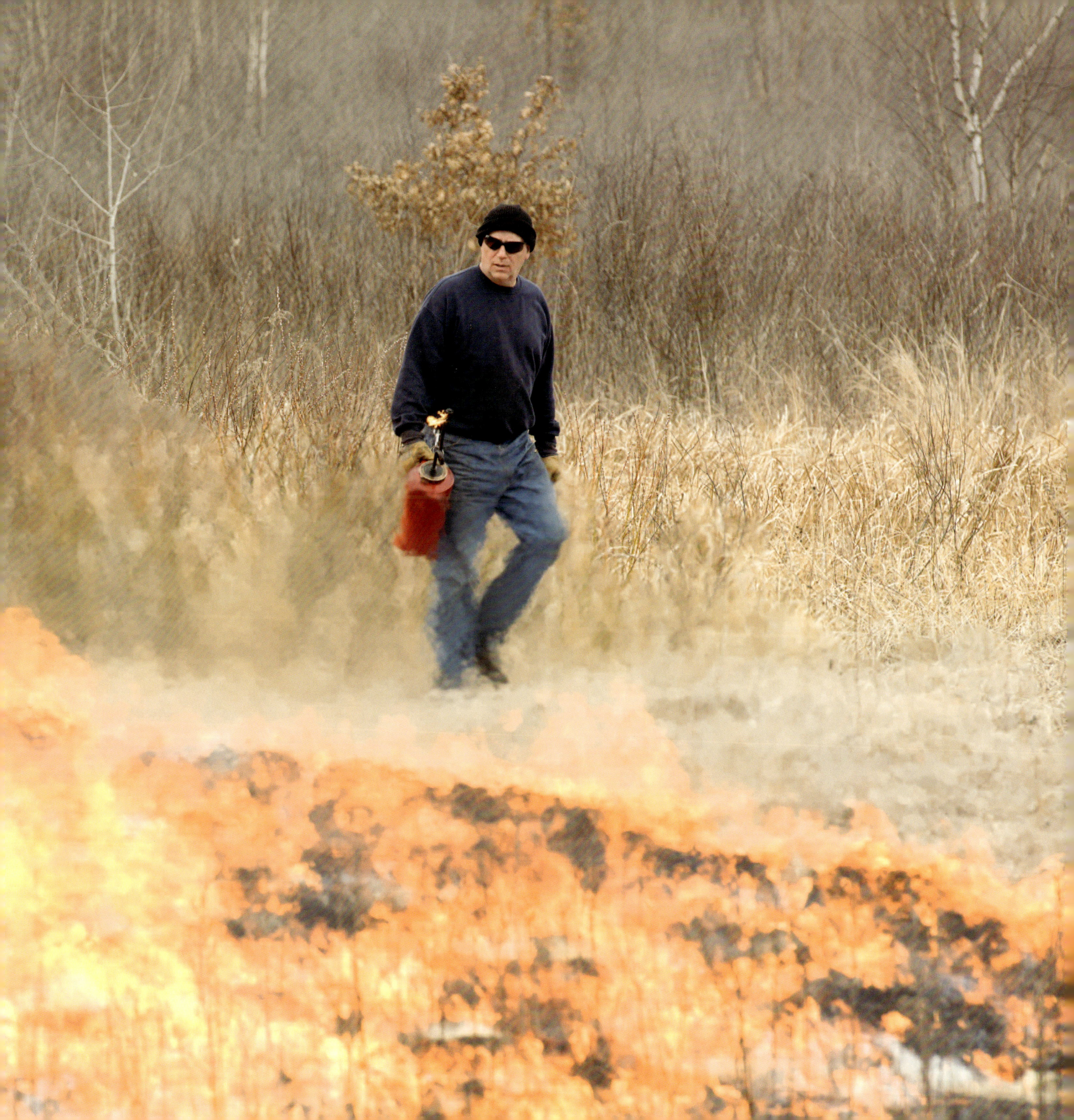

CHAPTER 5

The scorched earth smokes as the prairie grasses are engulfed in flames.

CHAPTER 5

Regenerated grasses come back to life, and birds such as northern flickers feed among the new growth.

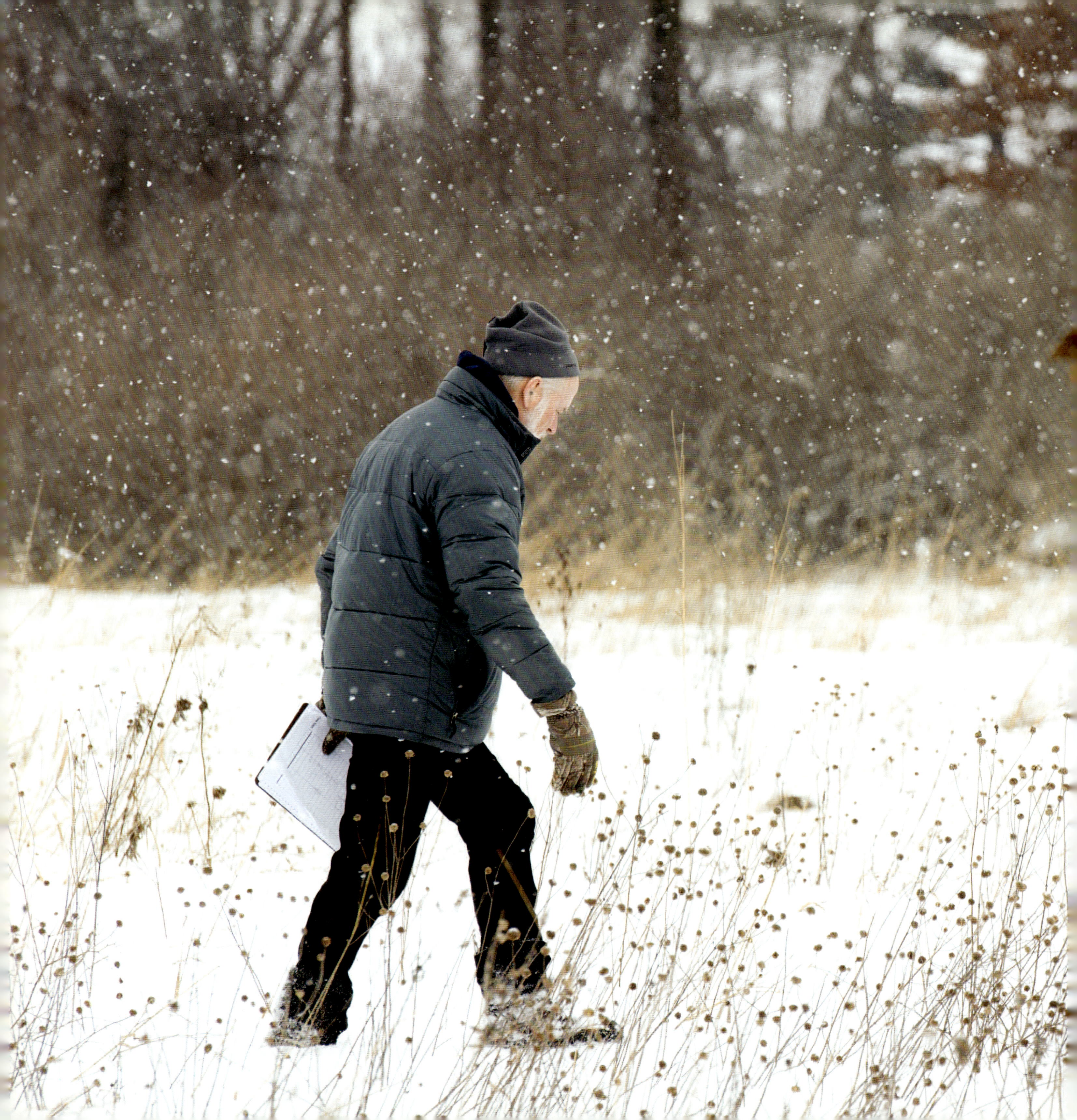

CHAPTER 5

Long-time director Larry Dolphin, set to retire in 2016, leads a prairie survey during a serene snowfall.

The setting sun bursts through the clouds for a brief moment before disappearing behind the horizon.

*The poetry of the earth
is never dead.*
—John Keats

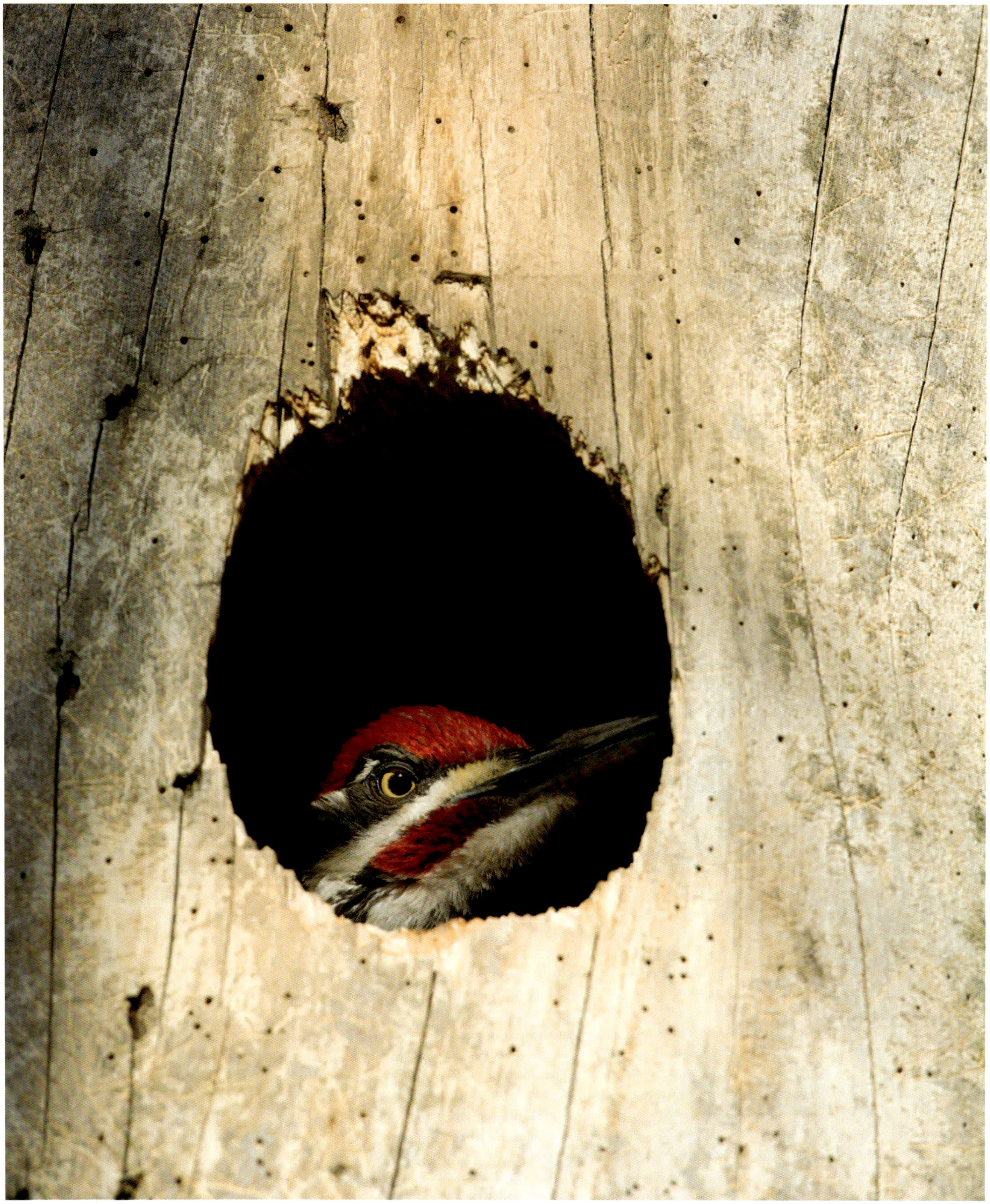

PHOTOGRAPHER'S NOTES

Every time I head out on the trail there is the possibility for the marvelous. The chance always exists that the light will stream perfectly through the forest canopy, illuminating a woodpecker, or that the sun will break through the clouds, sending down its last rays of warmth on an amber prairie. This possibility is what drives me. I want to see those things. I want to experience them. Most of all, I want to photograph them.

Here are some of the stories behind some of my favorite images. It is my hope that while reading this section you feel as if you were there, right beside me, as I was taking each picture. Every picture I take has a story behind it. Here are the stories of a few.

Pileated Woodpecker
While working on a photography project about the prairies and wetlands of Minnesota before I began this book, I received a phone call from the nature center. They excitedly told me that they had found the nesting cavity of a pileated woodpecker, the largest woodpecker in Minnesota. It had carved out a cavity in a tree not far from the pond, just off the trail. I quickly gathered my gear and took the short hike out to the site. When I arrived, I found the cavity, but there was no sign of the woodpecker. Regardless, I set up my tripod and fixed my lens on the large hole in the dead tree. Nothing happened. The afternoon sun was blocked by the trees; even if the woodpecker poked his head out, there would have been no light for the shot. I packed up and left.

Determined to get an image, I went back before dawn the next morning. As the sun rose I saw that the light was shining perfectly on the cavity, and if the woodpecker was there it would make for a nice image. I waited and still nothing happened. By now shadows were starting to show on the tree, and they would soon cover the cavity entirely. Without the sun, the image would be dull and flat. I was running out of time. But just then the woodpecker emerged ever so slightly from the tree, barely visible. The sun hit him perfectly. I fired off a series of images as he slowly went back inside. I returned to the tree a number of times, and each time the woodpecker made an appearance.

194

NOTES

NOTES

Wild Turkey

While working on this book I knew I needed an image of a turkey, and I was hoping to capture a tom (a male) in full display. Turkeys are creatures of the forest; it is their dwelling place, where they find their food and where they are protected, albeit slightly, from predators. The forest, then, was where I began. A week went by without any usable shots. I had seen the toms displaying, but each time they did, I had an obstructed view. There always seemed to be tree branches in-between my camera and the turkeys, and I was never able to get a clear, crisp image.

One day while I was not necessarily looking for them, I found a flock of four hens and a tom that were in a thin strip of pine forest just north of the pond. This stretch of forest was too thick with vegetation for me to get a clear shot, but to the north was a harvested cornfield and to the south, a prairie. My hope was that they would wander into one of these areas.

I stayed out of the forest, not wanting to startle the already displaying tom. I watched but kept my distance. The hens moved north. The tom followed. As the hens crossed into the cornfield, I tried to read where they were going. They seemed to be moving northeast across the field toward the West Prairie Loop. I made a quick decision and decided to move ahead of them, hunker down, and wait.

The turkeys continued moving on the same line I had guessed they would. The hens were picking at the previous year's harvest as the tom continued his display; they were coming right at me. I was in the perfect position and was sure I would get the shot.

But I was seen. One of the hens froze and looked straight into my lens. Sensing her fear, the others looked as well. The tom, however, continued to display. This seemed to lessen the anxiety of the hens, who continued feeding on the corn. Soon they were within range. The tom puffed up his feathers and put on a show right in front of my lens.

I captured a number of images that day and finally got the pictures I was hoping for. Actually they turned out better than what I had envisioned, which doesn't happen often. The displaying tom in all his splendor, surrounded by a background of harvested corn, made for some nice images. The photos remind me of a certain day in November.

NOTES

NOTES

Coyote

I had seen them in the same prairie for five straight days. There were two of them, a mating pair, slowly and deliberately moving through the grass, making their way from one grove of trees to another, no doubt looking for rodents or an unlucky rabbit along the way. They moved quietly, almost silently as the morning sun appeared on the horizon. As the sun emerged more fully, however, they were gone, hastily disappearing back into the forest to wait again until night, thus eluding my camera for yet another day.

Beyond the pond and its myriad of croaking frogs and singing waterfowl, beyond the vast and open West Prairie Loop, even beyond the observation tower, there is the nature center's northernmost prairie, the land of the coyote. To be sure, the coyotes had been to all of these places, perhaps stopping at the pond for a drink, pouncing on a vole in the West Prairie Loop, or passing by the observation tower en route to the Prairie Garden Loop. But if they had, I hadn't seen them. The closest I came to seeing a coyote was seeing a shadow, a ghost in the night, and thinking that perhaps it was one but never knowing for sure.

Then in May 2015 I found myself in this new, still unnamed prairie, bereft of trails and referred to as the prairie north of the tower. Not only was this the land of the coyote, but also the land of the bobolink and the dickcissel, prairie birds that had only arrived at the nature center after more land was purchased and restored as prairie habitat.

And so for five days I hiked through this new prairie, seeing a pair of coyotes each day, but each day coming home without an image. After the fifth day I decided to wake up earlier in the morning and hike to the prairie before the sun began to push the stars aside.

I arrived well before dawn, the only light coming from the moon and stars. After moving through the thick, wet grass, I picked a spot where I thought it was possible to see the coyotes, possible being the key word. I was not optimistic. The location I chose was the only area where I could get an image. While the rest of the prairie grasses were already taller than a coyote, this small stretch, close to the edge of the forest, was substantially shorter. And so I waited.

Just after first light, I heard a rustling sound coming from behind a thick clump of grasses. I turned my head and saw the grasses move ever so slightly. The sound was getting louder, and whatever was behind the grasses was coming closer. Then I saw it—a turkey. I didn't bother tripping the shutter as I already had enough images of turkeys, and soon it disappeared into the forest.

I continued waiting as the sun was close to peeking over the horizon. Just before it did, I saw a ghost—the coyote. I didn't even hear it approach. I looked up and it was there. I moved my head slowly and looked through the viewfinder—it was still there and it was moving closer. I couldn't contain my excitement as my heart raced and my hands shook. I tried to calm down, steady myself. A deep breath helped. All the while I never moved my eye from the viewfinder and never took my finger off the shutter button. I pressed the shutter: click. It came closer: click click. Closer still: click click click. I don't think it knew what I was. Remember, I was sitting on the ground with a large camera lens on a tripod in front of me. All the coyote saw was the front glass of the lens and the legs of the tripod. I was dressed in camouflage.

Ever so slowly it went back into the forest. I had 15 to 20 seconds with it, but that was enough. I had captured its image.

After waiting for another couple of minutes, I stood up, hoping to try to find it in the woods. When I stood, there was a loud rustling in the brush next to me, 10 yards away and to the left of where I was watching the coyote. I turned quickly and heard something running deep into the forest. I realized the coyote had flanked me and was watching me from the woods. It was a strange feeling to be stalked by a ghost.

198

NOTES

Trail

Everything looks different from 1,500 feet in the air. Objects that are big look small, distances that are long look short, and ecosystems that you think are substantial look minuscule. Flying in a small propeller plane, sitting next to the pilot with the window open, and my camera hanging above the earth puts things in perspective. The nature center is one of the few natural places in the area. Seeing it from above drives home the fact that so few places remain for wildlife.

I have hiked the trails at the nature center hundreds of times and have walked thousands of miles through its different ecosystems, but I had never seen it from the air. From above, the amber prairies in autumn are brilliant. I hoped to capture an image without any trees or brush to distract from the prairie itself. This was tricky. I had trouble shooting straight down because to do so I would need to unbuckle my seatbelt, stick my shoulders out the window, point my camera towards the earth, and shoot—which was not going to happen.

Instead, the pilot asked me how my stomach was. He was really asking if I would throw up if he banked the plane hard to the left. With my fingers crossed, I said no. Shortly thereafter he banked it, and I got the images that I was hoping for. And no, I did not throw up.

In this image you can see the main hiking trail going through the West Prairie. But if you look closely, you can see game trails that have been worn in as well. There are other aerial shots in the previous chapters, but this one is by far my favorite, perhaps because of how much I love the prairie.

NOTES

Sunset

Sunsets at the nature center always have the potential to be dramatic. Because of the way the landscape sits and where the sun dips below the horizon, dusk is a beautiful time to hike. In the fall, after a summer's worth of growth, grasses in the prairie can reach six- to-seven feet tall. This makes the prairie difficult to photograph.

When shooting landscapes, I prefer to shoot down from a higher vantage point, which allows for a greater sense of space in an image. This is important when photographing prairies that are flat. When land is flat, it is difficult to show its vastness.

This was my challenge while photographing the prairies at the nature center. There is a lot of flat land. Early in the summer this wasn't such an issue; I could shoot over the tops of the short grasses. But as the summer wore on and the grasses grew over my head, this became more of a test. I struggled to find the answer. I tried holding the camera above my head and snapping the shutter without looking through the viewfinder, but the results were crooked pictures.

Then at home one day I saw a ten-foot ladder. A light bulb went on in my head. I could use the ladder to rise above the prairie grasses. Why hadn't I thought about this before? It was perfect.

The next day I took the ladder to the nature center and hiked with it on my shoulders, my camera in my backpack. During the hike I realized I had underestimated the weight of the ladder. Or perhaps I had overestimated my own strength. I carried it on my five-mile hike, but it was so heavy that I was more concerned about my next step than my next shot. I couldn't concentrate on carrying the ladder and take pictures at the same time. The ladder went back in the shed.

When I returned it, I noticed a ladder that was only six feet tall and much lighter. Atop it I would be above the prairie grasses with plenty of room to spare. So I gave it a try.

The first time was on a windy day—not a good idea. I nearly fell off every time I got on. The next time, I set it up on a trail and started taking pictures of the sunset. I was so focused on the pictures that when a happy couple walked by, they scared the living daylights out of me. Again I almost fell.

The third time turned out to be the charm, and I was able to get some wonderful images of the sunset over the prairie. Persistence was the key. It would have been easy to give up after the first few failures. But nature photographers need both persistence and tenacity . . . and perhaps a few ladders.

NOTES

Monarch Butterfly

Late August is one of my favorite times of the year. The late summer prairie flowers are in full bloom, and the grasses start turning golden brown. The warm days are about to give way to crisp, cool, frosty mornings, and the forest will soon transition from summer green to different shades of orange, red, and yellow as the oaks, maples, and aspens prepare for winter. On the cusp of this change, monarch butterflies will begin their migration, heading south to the Sierra Madre mountain range in Mexico. How they know to migrate is an unanswered question, an ecological mystery. But migrate they must and it is a journey fit for the king of butterflies.

The nature center is listed as a Monarch Waystation, a natural area that can support these regal insects. In order for a monarch to survive, it needs different plants at different times in its life. A monarch butterfly will lay tiny, cream-colored eggs on the underside of milkweed plants, which are plentiful at the nature center. When the egg hatches and the caterpillar emerges, it consumes the egg and immediately begins feeding on milkweed leaves. Eventually it will grow large enough to form into a chrysalis and emerge as an adult monarch butterfly. As an adult it will no longer feed on milkweed leaves, as it does exclusively as a caterpillar; it will feed on the nectar from plants such as blazing star and goldenrod, both of which grace the nature center's prairies.

The Prairie Garden Loop's northeast corner is one of the best places to photograph monarchs. In August, blazing star is abundant and provides lovely contrasting colors as the monarchs feed on it. Areas closer to the visitor center offer photo-worthy scenes as well, but in the Prairie Garden Loop you are alone with the butterflies, undisturbed by traffic, buildings, and people. It is one of my favorite areas in the nature center, where a bit of the wild remains. It is a place where big bucks chase does during the rut, where coyotes hunt for voles, and where beautiful butterflies rest, refuel, and continue their journey south.

NOTES

NOTES

Wood Duck

In mid-April I found myself sitting in the mud. This was getting old. It also seemed like a waste of time. Why would I keep sitting here while I could be out searching for other things to photograph? It was a measurement of risk versus reward. The risk: potentially missing the opportunity to photograph other animals. The reward: the wood duck. This reward would take time. This reward was worth it.

Each spring thousands of birds migrate north from their wintering grounds in the south. Herons, egrets, geese, ducks, hawks, songbirds, and sandpipers all fly north to nest and raise their young. Some use the nature center as a resting place and continue on their journey. Some call it home. Canada geese and mallards usually nest somewhere near the pond. Wood ducks nest in tree cavities and use the pond to raise their young, but they do so secretly. If you go near the pond, they will quickly fly away. This makes them difficult to photograph. You can't approach them. You must wait.

So for two weeks I waited for the wood ducks. I built a homemade blind out of garden posts and camouflage fabric, and I sat in the mud, in the cattails, in the dark of the early morning, listening to the American woodcock peenting and twittering somewhere behind me. I sat on the north edge of the pond, waiting for the ducks to arrive. They came to the pond each morning, but never swam close enough. It was almost as if they could sense something was off.

After two weeks I switched tactics and locations. I went to the pond's south edge and sat, without a blind, amongst the vegetation, still in the mud. Just after dawn I heard a wood duck approach. He landed in the pond and moved through the shadows and came right at me. I focused my camera on him as he moved closer. Once he was within range, I pressed the shutter and took a series of images. He saw me but he didn't fly away. If I would have known it would be this easy, I wouldn't have bothered with the blind.

518 Acres of Forest, Prairie, and Pond

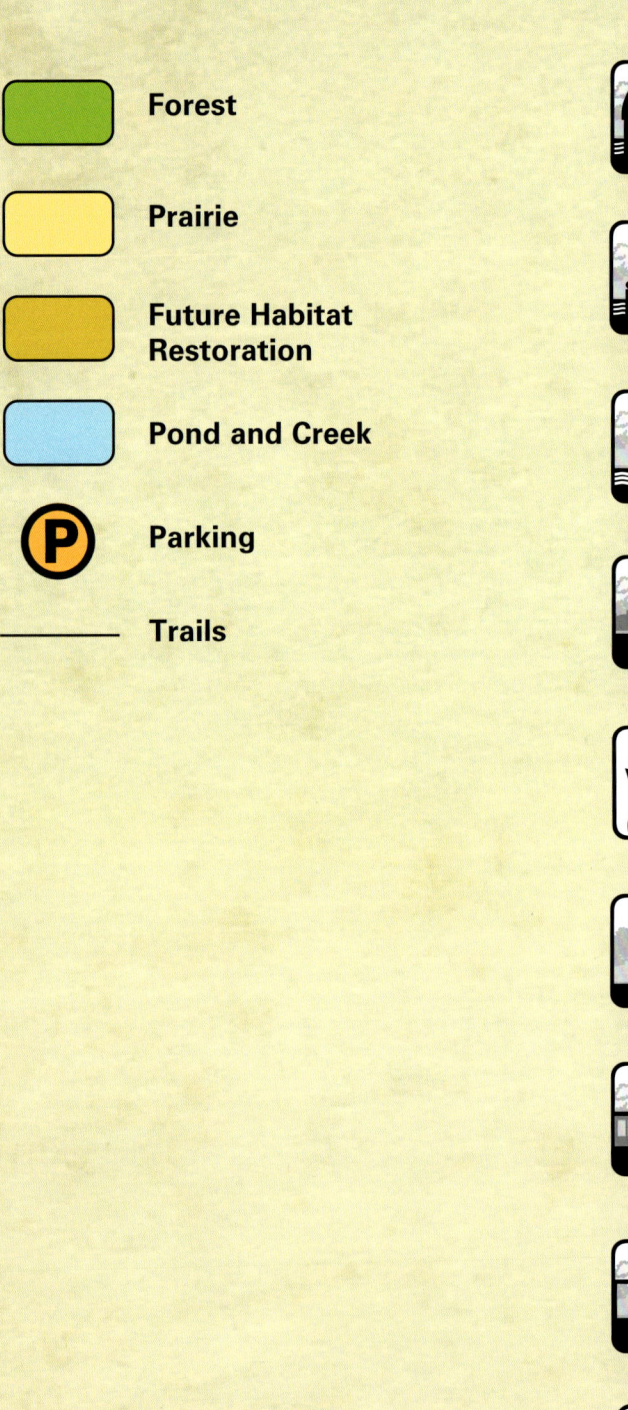

- Forest
- Prairie
- Future Habitat Restoration
- Pond and Creek
- Parking
- Trails

- Covered Bridge
- Bridges
- Stepping Stone Bridges
- Log Cabin
- Sugar Shack
- Tower
- Visitor Center
- Future Interpretive Center
- Ruby Rupner Auditorium
- Gerard Academy (Former home of Jay Hormel)

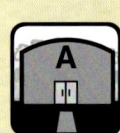

Jay C. Hormel Nature Center Trail Map

Back end sheets: Covered in snow from a recent winter storm, eastern hemlock trees stand tall near the South Trail.

Back cover: A raccoon emerges from the forest just before dusk.